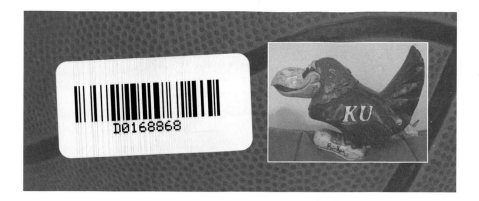

"Tyrel came in as a nervous kid – really nervous around me, and didn't get me at all for a while. As he matured and developed, he became one of the most fun kids to be around, period. He's almost too good. The only other kid we've had here like that would probably be Wayne Simien, who was almost too good to be true. Tyrel is a remarkable young man. He's one that, in his own way, in my opinion, at least midway through the (2010-11) season, was the face of our program."

– Bill Self, Kansas men's basketball coach

"It was a real pleasure for me to get to see him up close in my first six months here as the athletic director at KU. The best way to summarize it is, to me, Tyrel Reed represents all the best qualities that you would hope for in any student-athlete. On the court, in the classroom, as a person, someone you would want your son or daughter to emulate. I don't know that there's a greater compliment than that."

– Sheahon Zenger, Kansas athletic director

"Living with Tyrel was fun. Tyrel is always energetic; he's always upbeat. He never has a dull moment. There's always Dr. Pepper around. He probably singlehandedly keeps the Dr. Pepper company alive. We always got along so well. We still are great friends even after we've moved on."

– Cole Aldrich, Oklahoma City Thunder

"Therefore, since we are surrounded by such a great cloud of witnesses, let us throw off everything that hinders and the sin that so easily entangles, and let us run with perseverance the race marked out for us. " Hebrews 12:1

This verse epitomizes who Tyrel is as a man on and off the court. So much of his life has been brought into the spotlight, yet it is not what he has done in the eyes of the public, but rather the person he is when no one is watching. It is not what he has accomplished, but who he became while on the path of accomplishment. Anybody can argue that they are a team player or loyal, but only few can show they are relentless, tenacious, and accountable. Over his college career he has shown these characteristics. He does not focus on obstacles that may hinder him but fixes his eyes on the task at hand with determination and perseverance. In college basketball, the seasons can be tough physically, mentally, and especially academically. There are many times he played hurt or had a big exam the next day and he would find a way not only to be successful but to exceed expectations. It is an honor and a privilege to be a friend and brother to a man who is full of courage and integrity. "

— *Darrell Stuckey, San Diego Chargers (and brother in-law)*

REED

ALL ABOUT IT:
DRIVEN TO BE A JAYHAWK

by *TYREL REED*
with Tully Corcoran

FOREWORD BY COLE ALDRICH

www.ascendbooks.com

Requests for permission should be addressed to Ascend Books, LLC, Attn: Rights and
Permissions Department, 10101 W. 87th Street, Suite 200, Overland Park, KS 66212.

Photo Credits: Kansas Athletics, Jeff Jacobsen – Cover photos, pages 1,10,11,
39,55,101,140,144, 160,161,162,163,164, 165,166,167,168,169,170,171,172,
173,174,175, 206,208,209,217,235,237
Photos on page 226 and 229 were used with permission from the Voo Verviers Pepinster.
Photo Credit: Bob Snodgrass – page 34
All other photos are from the Reed Family's personal collection.

Every reasonable attempt has been made to determine the ownership of copyright.
Please notify the publisher of any erroneous credits or omissions, and corrections
will be made to subsequent editions/future printings.

10 9 8 7 6 5 4 3 2 1

This book is not an official publication of, nor is it endorsed by, the University of Kansas.

Printed in the United States of America

ISBN-978-0-9836952-0-2

Library of Congress Cataloging-in-Publications Data Available Upon Request

Editor: Lee Stuart and Cindy Ratcliff
Cover Design and Interior Page Design: Lynette Ubel
Publication Coordinator: Christine Drummond

www.ascendbooks.com

REED
ALL ABOUT IT:
DRIVEN TO BE A JAYHAWK

by **TYREL REED**
with Tully Corcoran

FOREWORD BY COLE ALDRICH

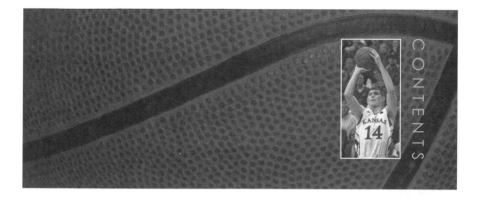

CONTENTS

ACKNOWLEDGEMENT

Anybody who followed my career in college knows I'm not a big talker, especially when it comes to talking about myself.

So maybe it seems weird I have written a book about, you know, myself. Truthfully, it isn't something I would have come up with on my own, but when the people at Ascend Books contacted me about doing it, and I thought about what I could share, it occurred to me that there are thousands of kids all over the state of Kansas just like me. Kids who dream of putting on that Kansas jersey and running out of the tunnel and making a big shot against Missouri. I wanted to tell my story for those kids, so they could see that if they work hard and trust in themselves and do the right thing, it is possible to live that dream, even if you are from a small town.

First and foremost, I want to thank the Lord for everything he has done in my life and for putting me in the position I am now in. I want to thank my wife, Jessica, my parents, my sister, Lacie, my friends and teammates, all of my coaches, from Coach Self and all the assistants to my AAU coach, L.J. Goolsby, to my high school coach (my dad) and everybody who coached me as a kid.

I'd also like to thank the people at Ascend Books, Bob Snodgrass and Christine Drummond, who organized it all, my co-author, Tully Corcoran, who helped me write the book, and Lee Stuart, who edited it.

Finally, I want to thank the Jayhawk Nation, and all the people who supported me along the way. You made my career special, and if it weren't for you, this book wouldn't exist.

FOREWORD

By Cole Aldrich, former Kansas Jayhawk and current member of the Oklahoma City Thunder of the NBA

It was our first day as college kids. Summer school at Kansas.

Tyrel will tell a story about me that day. He will tell you a story about how I wore a wife-beater shirt to class, and how Coach Self happened to be driving by and scolded me for it. His version of this story is probably true, and it probably helps explain me a little bit.

But I have a story from that very same day about Tyrel, which will help explain him even more.

I didn't really know him then. We had played against each other in AAU ball, I think, but we didn't know each other. I knew he was my roommate and that he was from Kansas, and that was about it.

Well, the first day of school, he sent me a text saying he had found a dollar on the sidewalk on the way to class. He was totally pumped about it.

Tyrel, you might say, is "thrifty." I always make fun of him for it, but it's a good trait.

He and I do a lot of that with each other. He gives me crap, I give him crap. It's give-and-take. I always called him the most athletic un-athletic guy I'd ever seen. He hated that. He was so athletic, but he would never try to dunk on anybody. In turn, he makes fun of my golf swing. It would be stuff like that. We got along well as roommates because we are pretty similar. We approach life in similar ways. Even though I'm from a much bigger city, I think we had similar sensibilities. But we were just different enough. I think I might have helped him become more outgoing and more independent. What I got from him was somebody who was always there. A great friend.

It helped, too, that neither of us was really interested in going out and raising hell. Going to school we were both nervous, hoping and praying we were going to have a good roommate we liked. That's what got Tyrel and me through our freshman year, going through those things and being there for each other. If we would have had roommates going out and doing different things, I don't know if we would have been as close. Usually if we were up at 3 a.m., we were playing X-Box.

He and I spent countless hours in our dorm room, talking about things. We came in together as freshmen, and struggled through that together, each in our own way. Both of us got criticized pretty hard from Coach Self that year, and that's a difficult thing to deal with. I was playing in the games a little more, and Tyrel was getting it a little more in practice, but we both were going through that.

Tyrel was always there for me, and I think I helped pull him out of his shell a little bit.

Tyrel's such a perfectionist, he takes criticism really hard. He was terrified of Coach Self that first year. I told him many times not to take things personally, and eventually he got past that. But Tyrel is a pleaser, and he hates to feel like someone is disappointed in him.

I think that is what has made him the player and the person he became. He is all about details. He is a perfectionist.

I know Tyrel is going to keep playing basketball for a while, but I really think he could do anything. Over the time that I've known him as a basketball player, he has grown so much. It proves he can do whatever he wants to do. He's going to put his mind to it and excel.

I can do all this
through him who gives
me strength.

Philippians 4:13

The National Championship Game

CHAPTER 1

To this day, whenever I hear the song "Beat It" by Michael Jackson, it reminds me of sitting on the team bus on the way to the Alamodome in San Antonio to play Memphis for the national championship.

I don't know why I remember that because I have a terrible memory and, to be honest, until I began working on this book, I had not spent a lot of time reflecting on our 2008 national championship. I still have never watched a tape of the entire game.

Also, although I consider Michael Jackson to be among the greatest entertainers of all time and would certainly attend a Michael Jackson concert if he were still alive, I'm really more of a Garth Brooks fan.

Yet my iPod selected MJ during that bus ride, so in my head the soundtrack to the 2008 national championship game begins with "Beat It" and ends with "One Shining Moment."

So many of the things my mind chose to remember about that night are totally random. For example, I don't remember the Memphis roster all that well. I know we were focused on stopping

Derrick Rose – Coach Self always says if you cut off the head, the body will follow – and we were confident in stopping Chris Douglas-Roberts. I remember Robert Dozier and Joey Dorsey, but there are probably a lot of fans who could tell you the names on that team better than I could. On the other hand, I remember that for the North Carolina game two days earlier, Walt Aldrich, Cole's dad, was wearing jean shorts and a Cole Aldrich jersey with nothing underneath it. I remember us always talking about Walt wearing that jersey with those jean shorts.

The day of the championship game began the way most road game days began that year. I woke up sweaty in my sweltering hotel room with Sherron Collins, who was my roommate for road games that year. For some reason, Sherron loved to keep his room hot. And I hate my room hot. I have to sleep in some cool air. If I had to sleep in an igloo, I'd be fine, just pull as many covers as I need. But it was a hot box in there. I remember sweating every night in the room. It was probably 80 degrees when we slept, and he sleeps under the covers. I don't know how he does it. It was like a sauna. It was kind of miserable, but he was the upper classman. I had no say. I just kind of went along with it. I'm a pretty easy-going guy, and I can deal with it, but that sucked.

There was really no exact science to how our coaches split up our rooms on the road. They kind of just put you with somebody. Sherron and I got along great. It is different with your roommates in the Jayhawker Towers on campus, though. Coach Self tries to put people together who are gonna mesh well. You don't want to put two guys together who are maybe gonna get in trouble all the time. You want to put the people who balance each other out and are gonna get along the most. He's great with managing personalities.

My roommate in the dorms was Cole, and it worked out great. He was a kid from Minnesota, and he was from a lot bigger city, but he was kind of a weird, country boy at heart. Down to earth. That's kinda how I am, so it was really easy for us to get along.

Cole was kind of a weird, country boy at heart.

Something most people probably wouldn't realize is just how much time we spend in our hotel rooms on the road. Basically, if we aren't at the gym, eating a team meal, or traveling, we are in the hotel room. We pretty much do what you'd expect. Sherron loved to talk on the phone, so most of the time he would be on the phone with friends from back in Chicago or whoever. Sometimes we would watch a movie, watch ESPN, mess around on the Internet, check Facebook. Everything you would expect.

I like to read a lot of news. I get pretty bored with ESPN after a while, so I would usually end up on the computer, checking CNN.com just to keep up with what's happening in the world. I can do that all day.

That doesn't make all of this fun.

That Final Four, I think I had cabin fever the worst I've ever had in my life. If we weren't at the gym, we were in our hotel room the entire time. You're down there for like a week. You may get to say hi to your mom or dad in the lobby for five minutes when you're coming back from a shootaround, and even that is only if they're there. I had pretty much no contact with them face to face. I would talk to them on the phone a little bit before going to bed. Same with my girlfriend. I just talked to her on the phone. The only time I saw her was when we had kind of a little family get-together where everyone's families came up to one of those conference rooms at the top of the hotel. She came with my parents and my sister.

It's really tough for us. I remember one day, right outside our hotel, Taylor Swift and Kid Rock were playing a concert. I literally could hear them playing. My mom and my sister called to tell me, "Hey, we're down at the concert." And this sucks for me. I can hear this concert and my family is right down there, but I can't go.

— ◆ —

Tyrel's family enjoyed the week, although unlike Tyrel and the rest of the players, they weren't exactly in luxury accommodations.

They had more fun anyway.

"We drove down with a couple of my coaching buddies and one of their sons," said Stacy Reed, Tyrel's father. "They were going to buy tickets when they got there. We got two rooms at a cheap hotel. We had to walk about six or eight blocks to get to the River Walk. I caught a basketball Dick Vitale threw out when he was riding a boat on the River Walk. I had him sign the basketball. We went to the Alamo that day. I'm a history and government teacher. When I travel I always want to do a lot of those history type things."

That part of it, he couldn't share with his son.

"We had a great experience," he said. "I felt bad for Tyrel. They don't get to do anything. I was the one getting to do it."

— ◆ —

It's all about distractions. If we're not holed up, not in our rooms all the time, people are going to be wanting autographs and asking for pictures. There's just a lot of things you don't want to have to be dealing with. Guys don't want to be out shopping at the mall or doing whatever we do as college kids. We need to be focused.

The national championship game always starts late in the evening, so we didn't need to get up early that day. We woke up about 10 a.m. and had a team breakfast about 10:30 that morning. Coach Self knows we're college kids and don't enjoy getting up. When we can and when we're able to, he's willing to let us sleep in a little bit. Our shootaround was at 11:30 a.m.

Normally, our gameday shootarounds go for about 45 minutes, and they're intense. We use it as a chance to get better, not just to put some shots up. If you don't practice well at the shootaround, you could end up running. We take them seriously. But the shootaround that day was the shortest we ever had. It probably lasted 15 minutes, maybe less. Coach Self just knew that we were going to be ready to play.

I was not a regular part of the rotation at this point, so I played on the scout team. Your role as a scout team player in practice is to replicate as closely as possible a player from the opposing team. It's all about working on the scouting report. For example, if you were playing Baylor, someone would be LaceDarius Dunn and that guy would take a bunch of deep three-pointers.

Well, at this practice, I was Derrick Rose, Memphis' freshman point guard who ended up being the No. 1 pick in the NBA draft a couple of months later. I had his number on. I was D-Rose. I wasn't quite the same player he was at that time, but I did my best. My game was not like his. I usually shot a lot of three-pointers, whereas Derrick was a slasher. So I'm playing out of character, going off the dribble, trying to beat Mario Chalmers.

I remember hitting a driving shot off the glass during that practice and thinking maybe I should act like I'm D-Rose more often. Mario Chalmers was guarding me and I took him off the dribble because that's what Rose does. He was really good off the dribble. I did a step-back and I hit it off the glass. I hadn't done anything like that in a while.

I'm thinking maybe I should act like I'm D-Rose more often.

Thinking back to this is kind of funny because Derrick ended up banking in a shot against us that night, and it was probably the biggest shot of the game for Memphis. I guess I had been a pretty accurate scout.

After the shootaround, we grab some lunch and it's back to the hotel again. I remember in the hotel room with Sherron, watching ESPN and hearing Jay Bilas' picks and whoever else. We knew most people thought Memphis was the better team, but we felt like we were going to win. That group of guys had been through so much and the year before had gotten so close to the Final Four, then lost to UCLA. It just felt like it was our turn now, it was our time. It's like fuel to our fire. Yeah, they had lost only one game, but still. We just felt like we were more experienced, and just a better team, regardless of what anybody else was saying. I think our whole locker room was saying, man, let's go prove to these guys that we are the best.

There was no doubt in our minds we were gonna win that game. We had gotten so far, we played so well against North Carolina. We felt like the momentum was with us and that was our time.

I think when you're a basketball player, you obviously think you're gonna win every game. That's the mentality you should have. Playing at Kansas, that's what we expected. There was not a game that we played where we thought a team was better than we were. When we did lose, we just felt like maybe they had outplayed us that day. Any given day, we should beat any team. That was our mindset going in. We were just excited to have that opportunity.

Really, this was part of the reason our shootaround was so short. That group of guys was so experienced. Coach Self knew we were gonna be ready to play. We were gonna get to the point and we were gonna get out of there. Nothing else needs to be done. No need to waste any added energy on that. There's gonna be enough energy to expend that night, we didn't need to put it into that shootaround. Our coaches stay up all night going over scouting reports and everything. They're so prepared for the game and they have everything to tell us. For us, we just want the game to come. We don't want to hear any more scouting reports.

That group of guys was so mature. The core of that team was basically juniors and seniors: Russell Robinson, Darnell Jackson and Sasha Kaun, plus Brandon Rush and Mario with Sherron and Shady (Darrell Arthur) as sophomores. We didn't have an obvious, definable leader, but as a guard the guy I always watched was Russ Rob.

He was so calm all day. All of them were. They had been around. They'd gotten knocked out in the first round when they were freshmen. Got a little bit better when they were sophomores and juniors. They were just extremely calm, going about it as a regular game. We were obviously pumped up and extra amped, but those guys weren't nervous, they were just going about their business, acting like it was a regular basketball game.

Our game plan wasn't that complicated. We knew there were two important matchups on the perimeter with Rose and Chris Douglas-Roberts. CDR was having a great season. He was long and athletic and just did a little bit of everything, but we had Brandon Rush, who was the same size, just as athletic and a great defender. We felt like Brandon was a perfect matchup for him.

The Rose matchup wasn't so obvious. All the guards wanted a shot at him. Russ Rob, Mario, and Sherron all wanted a piece of him. There was no backing down. Sherron being from Chicago, where Rose was from, made Sherron really amped up to play that game. There was Dozier and Joey Dorsey, and Dorsey was a specimen of an athlete. But so was Sasha. Sasha is one of the strongest guys I've gone up against. We used to just beat the living heck out of him in practice. He would never complain about a foul. Never complain. We would just hammer him every day. My freshman year in practice, he'd have the ball on the block. When you're a guard you're supposed to dig down, and I'd swipe as hard as I could at the ball. It would hurt my arm, but he'd still have the ball.

Strongest dude ever. You could literally punch him in the head and draw blood and he wouldn't call a foul. Just the toughest guy who was always in it for everyone else and not himself. He was a rock. He was Ivan Drago from the Rocky movies, just a little bit taller.

You could literally punch Sasha in the head and draw blood and he wouldn't call a foul.

So I just didn't see where Memphis was going to have some great advantage. I felt like every person on that team, we matched up great against. Besides, we were the best defensive team in the country that year. We knew Memphis was going to try to get out and run, and we loved to run, too, but we could also slow it down and play a half-court game. We felt like we had an advantage there.

I think we were more focused on D-Rose than we were on CDR. We knew D-Rose made that team go. We had a bunch of guys who were ready and wanted to step up to the challenge of guarding him. As they say, defense wins championships, and I think our guys really did believe that. We were a great team defensively. Russ Rob set the tone every game, and being the great defensive player that he was, it just made everyone locked in that much more every time we stepped on the court.

Personally, I pretty much knew I wasn't going to play that night. You play in the national title game, you're going with your best, most experienced guys, and the rotation was pretty well established. I averaged six minutes per game that year. But still, you never completely know. Just before halftime of our Sweet 16 game, Coach Self had put Jeremy Case and me in for a few seconds just to get some shooters on the floor. Jeremy ended up making a three just before halftime. You always have to be ready for things like that.

A couple times during that tournament, against UNLV and North Carolina, I ended up with the ball to dribble out the final seconds. Now, you would probably never think this moment could be entertaining in any way, but everybody thought this was hilarious.

Let me explain.

When you're an inexperienced player and you don't know what to do, you usually just start dribbling. It's something most players do, and it's usually a sign of immaturity. Well, I did this all the time as a freshman. In practice, we'd be running something, and offense is all about timing. You get the ball, you pass it. Keep it moving. But since I was a little unsure sometimes, I would often start dribbling it.

Coach Self started calling me High School Hondo because of that. As in, "Hey, High School Hondo, what are you doing? Why are you dribbling so much?" He was always giving me crap about that.

So, fitting as it may have been, I ended up with the ball in the closing seconds of the UNLV game and we're just running out the clock. So I stood there and dribbled it until the time ran out. Well, Coach Self thought this was hilarious. Of course I would just start dribbling.

By the time we got on the bus after the game, we already had a DVD of the game. We popped it in and at the end, we're watching this and literally everyone on the bus is counting out loud the number of dribbles I made. I dribbled it something like 24 times in 18 seconds and with every bounce, all my teammates are going, "One! Two! Three!" and so on.

Well, this happens again in the North Carolina game. And, I mean, what am I going to do, just stand there and get a five-second violation called on me? So I started dribbling and I never heard the end of it. When the clock ran out, I gave Jeremy Case the ball. I think he still has that ball to this day. I don't know how he got it. He probably just put it in his bag and didn't tell anybody.

My point is, even though I knew I probably wasn't going to play at all, it's not like I could relax and just watch the game like the fan I had been my whole life. Because if I did get in, even if it was just for a couple seconds at the end of the first half, or for a few seconds to run off the last ticks on the clock, there was going to be some pressure to get it right.

Anyway, we were all so excited for the game to start. We had our pregame meal about four hours before the game, and got to the arena a couple hours before tip. Coach Self likes for us to have some down time at the arena. So guys are doing whatever they need to have done. If you need stretched out, you go to Andrea Hudy, our strength and conditioning coach, and she stretches you out. If you have a cut or a blister that needs to be treated, you go see Bill Cowgill, the team doctor. Everybody calls him "Cheddar," like the character Cheddar Bob from Eminem's movie 8-Mile. Wayne Simien came up with that when he was a player. Basically, Bill is a white guy hanging around with a bunch of black guys, so Wayne started calling him Cheddar. All the coaches call him that, too, but I don't think they know why.

Once we're in the locker room, we put on everything except our jerseys. Most of us didn't put on our jerseys until a few minutes before tip, when we run out of the tunnel for the last time. But until then, you just put on your shoes and shorts and warm-ups and go out for what we call NBA shooting, which is that shooting you've seen if you've ever been to a game. Guys out there, putting up some shots, kind of doing their own thing.

With the exception of the short shootaround, everything that day was exactly like a normal gameday, right up until that moment when we're putting on the jerseys. Five minutes before the game, you put your jersey on, and then it hits you that it's time. We waited all year for this exact moment where we come out and play. It's like, wow, it's finally here, let's go. Let's go take this, boys.

We knew it was going to be a great game. We wanted it to be a great game. In the Big 12 Tournament championship game that year, we beat Texas in a fantastic back-and-forth game. Both teams played great. We were expecting something like that out of the Memphis game.

For the most part, the first half went like we wanted it to go. Memphis got a nice early lead on us, but we weren't worried about that. It had been back and forth, but we led by five at halftime and felt like we had done what we wanted to do. I just felt like we were playing our game and it was going as planned. We definitely wanted to control the ball and keep them out of transition and we had mostly done that. We did a good job playing to the scouting report and had played good defense.

Derrick Rose had three points in the first half. Chris Douglas-Roberts had 13. We had planned on having Russell guard Rose because Russell was our best on-ball defender, but he picked up his second foul early and ended up playing only nine minutes in the first half. That meant Mario and Sherron got their chance to check him, and they did a pretty good job.

That was a good first half for us. But, of course, you can't win a game in the first half.

You always expect there to be a couple of big runs in any basketball game between good teams. It's unusual for the momentum to not shift two or three times and there was no question the momentum shifted pretty dramatically in Memphis' favor midway through the second half. Rose started taking over. He scored 15 in the second half (Douglas-Roberts scored three) and Memphis went as he went.

— ◆ —

Kansas was up by one with nine minutes left when Memphis made its move. Rose hit a three-pointer with 8:12 to play, then another jumper at 7:37, then an and-one play at 5:10, then a fall-away shot-clock-beating bank shot that, as it went in, CBS play-by-play man Jim Nantz described as "the shot of the tournament."

Between the 8:12 mark and the 2:37 mark, Rose scored all of Memphis' points, going on a personal 10-4 run that left Memphis with a 58-51 lead.

Rose's bank shot was initially ruled a three-pointer and later corrected to a two. It gave Memphis a seven-point lead and, as Reed points out, was a crushing blow. Kansas would trail by nine with 2:12 to play.

—◆—

I didn't think the game was over, but I thought, "Man, that's a dagger." Basketball has its ups and downs. When you see somebody make a shot like that, you get that feeling that it might be their day. As much as you shoot a basketball and practice, sometimes it's not your day and sometimes you can't miss. I put my head in my hands, looking down at the ground like, "that's tough."

—◆—

Except for Mario Chalmers, there might not have been a cooler head in the building than that of Lacie Reed, Tyrel's sister and a sophomore manager for the basketball team at the time.

Lacie was seated a few rows behind the KU bench and remembers experiencing total confidence Kansas would win the game.

"One of the other managers was freaking out, and I was like, 'I'm feeling good about this game,'" Lacie said. "Even when we were down, I was saying, 'It's going to be OK. We're going to come back.'"

With 2:12 left we took a timeout, and there was no panic in the huddle. I've seen panic before. Just worrying there is not enough time to come back.

But there was no panic. We've got this, we're still fine, we're still fine. I think those guys were so mature. It just seemed like from then on, it was our game.

I don't remember everything, but Shady started it off with a jumper and we started to make some plays. Once you start seeing that, when you start seeing a comeback, you start seeing a little bit of hope and you're just thinking, we can do this."

—◆—

The sequence was as follows:

Arthur made a jumper with 1:56 left to cut the Memphis lead to seven and Kansas immediately called timeout to set up a press on the inbounds play. Collins made a steal and on his way out of bounds, flung it back inbounds to Robinson, who drove to the basket looking to shoot but got stopped. He turned and passed it back to Collins, who had come back in bounds into the corner for a three-pointer to make it a four-point game with 1:46 left. The teams traded free throws, then, after a miss by Douglas-Roberts, Arthur made another jumper with 1:01 left to make it 62-60, Memphis.

Kansas then made a pair of mistakes. This was the first: With 27 seconds left, the Jayhawks forced a miss by Douglas-Roberts. Collins got the rebound and went racing up the floor. As he went to the basket for what would have been a game-tying layup, Memphis stole it and suddenly had the ball and a two-point lead with 19 seconds left. The second mistake was this: Kansas fouled Douglas-Roberts with 16 seconds left, hoping for at least one miss. He missed them both, but Dorsey got past Arthur for the rebound and got the ball out to Rose, whom KU immediately fouled.

Now the Jayhawks were hoping, again, for at least one missed free throw. Rose missed the first and made the second, putting Memphis up 63-60 with 10 seconds left.

Without a timeout, KU inbounded the ball to Collins.

—◆—

Chop

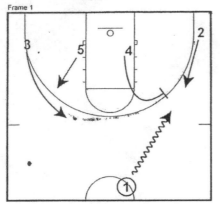

Frame 1

In half-court situation we start in 1-4 flat. 1 speed dribbles to the wing.

Frame 2

DHO into immediate ballscreen. 3 comes off weakside flare screen.

Frame 3

4 & 5 set downscreen & pop or slip depending on if we need a 2 or a 3.

Frame 4

BACKDOOR OPTION: 2 goes backdoor. 1 uses ballscreen by 4. Everything else stays the same.

It seemed surreal when Derrick Rose missed that free throw and gave us that opportunity. In our minds, we knew that now we've got a chance.

We were running a play called "Chop." It's one of those plays that we ran a thousand times and people knew exactly what we're going to do, but it's a tough play to guard. It's the one we always ran in late-clock situations, where the guards hand off the ball on the perimeter. Coach Self just makes a chopping motion with his hands and that's it.

The point guard brings it down and has the option to pitch it back or take it to the basket. We needed a three at that time so we pitched it back.

Sherron was falling down and I don't know how he got that pass off. He kind of threw it over his shoulder. That wasn't supposed to happen. Meanwhile, on the other side of the court, one of our bigs is setting a fade screen for the other guard on that side. It would have been Brandon Rush. So once he catches the ball from Sherron, Mario can throw a fade screen pass to Brandon for the three in the corner. I think we all knew it wasn't gonna happen. Mario had hit big shot after big shot. He had done that countless times throughout his career, so we had the confidence he was going to come off and knock it down.

Mentally, Mario was unique in that he never worried about mistakes. He was the best I've ever played with when it came to that. He never let a bad play affect him. I truly mean that. Of all the guys I've ever played with he was the best at, say, making a turnover and not thinking about it again. I was a little bit of the opposite. I would live in the past, like, man I made a turnover, that hurts. That cost us a possession. I'd relive it. You shouldn't be that way. I got better as I got older. Coach Self says it should be water off your back. I completely agree with that. But that's what made Mario so clutch. He had that uncanny ability to just let things go. He didn't care what people would have said if he had missed it. It didn't even occur to him he might miss. He expected to make it, and most of the time he did.

As soon as the shot went through, we knew it was over. We still had to go to overtime, but we had all the momentum. Memphis was just so deflated.

—◆—

Lacie's confidence had been rewarded.

"We started coming back and the other manager was like, 'You're right! You're right!'" she said. "When Mario's shot went up I knew it was going in. It was funny, I felt so calm about that game and everybody else was freaking out."

In the stands, Stacy remembers Tyrel walking over after the game and not saying much.

"With he and I, it's just eye contact," Stacy said. "That's all we need. What an experience for Lacie, being there. How lucky a parent am I? My daughter is there, my son is there. I got to live this."

— ◆ —

After the game, we get eight minutes to ourselves before the media comes in for interviews. It was just complete and utter joy. Coach came in there and told us how much he loved us, how much he was so proud of us and how he knew all along we were going to get this done. It was the perfect culmination. I can't even explain how great it had to feel for Russ Rob and the rest of those guys, in your last year of college, to win the national championship. That had to be amazing.

The final score gets forgotten pretty quickly, but I'll bet a lot of KU fans remember that one.

Everybody kept going up to Mario and rubbing him on the head, telling him they loved him for making that shot.

So we were all in there laughing and celebrating and enjoying the moment. I remember Mario sitting there almost like nothing had even happened. He was so calm. Everybody kept going up to him and rubbing him on the head, telling him they loved him for making that shot. And he was just sitting in his chair. I think we were all happier for him than he was for himself. He was kind of like, well, I've done that before and I'll do that again. Sitting there as calm, cool, collected as anybody I've ever seen. It was funny to see somebody like that. That's how he did his whole career. He never got too high or too low.

Cole's a very emotional, funny type of dude. He was just celebrating, jumping up and down, laughing. Sherron loves to celebrate, jump up

My family and I have always been really close. It was such a blessing to get to share that night with them.

and down, have a good time. I'm kind of reserved. Brady Morningstar is kind of intermediate. Probably the person who had the most fun was Sasha, and you could never understand him, anyway. It was funny to see this big, 6'11" Russian guy bouncing around like that. Ivan Drago and all.

So we were all in there being kids, celebrating, and then our sports information director, Chris Theisen, opens the locker room doors for all the media to come in. It's important for us to be professional when we're with the media. Every year before the season, we have a professional come in and teach us how to deal with the media. There isn't a lot to it. It lasts only thirty or forty-five minutes, but they teach you to be polite, not to say "um" a million times, not to ever say "no comment" – saying that just makes things seem worse – not to give another team bulletin board material. The main thing is just being smart.

So when they come in, we're trying to put on our professional faces. We don't really want to do it. We would always give Chris a hard time, telling him not to open the door. But it's just part of playing college basketball.

The media session after that game was ridiculous. We were in there for at least an hour. I couldn't even have counted how many people were in front of Mario. There were a few people in front of me. They probably couldn't get to Mario so they just settled for me.

After that, it was back to the team hotel (again). We probably got back about 1 a.m. We had an entire floor to ourselves. The national championship trophy was up there and there was a bunch of food and drinks for everybody. We basically hadn't seen our families or friends at all that week, and they all got to come up and celebrate with us. My girlfriend, Jessica, was there. Everybody sort of came and went as they pleased. Everybody was in the best mood. It was so rewarding. My family and I took a picture with the trophy.

— ◆ —

Getting back to the hotel, though, meant packing up all the equipment and loading it onto the bus.

Guess whose job that was?

"I wasn't at the top of the food chain," Lacie said.

Part of Lacie's role that night was to load the bus. The problem was that in her jeans and T-shirt, she didn't necessarily look like she belonged on the KU team bus, and encountered a skeptical security guard.

"This cop started yelling at us, like, 'You need to step away! I need to see your badges,' she said. "I was like, 'We're just trying to do our jobs and we're going to get in trouble.'"

— ◆ —

It was such a cool moment. I had grown up in Kansas and I lived and died with the Jayhawks. I remember in 2003 (when Kansas played Syracuse), watching Carmelo Anthony and seeing Hakim Warrick blocking Mike Lee's shot at the end of that championship game. I remember the Bucknell loss. We threw it the full length of the court and Wayne got it at the free throw line and I was sure it was going in. When I was a fan, it always felt like, "Why can't we ever get it done? It looks so easy. We were so good during the whole season and we can't get it done." Then we actually won. Finally, we got it done and I was a part of it. What cooler thing could have happened?

When we were in the locker room after the game but before the media came in, when it was just us, I remember sitting next to the other freshmen. It was Cole, Conner Teahan, Chase Buford, and me. We spent a lot of time together. I had a moment to myself and I just looked down, closed my eyes and thanked the Lord for what he had done for me, saying "Lord, thank you so much for getting me to this point in my life." I never would have expected I would be a Kansas Jayhawk and winning a national championship.

I don't think any of us got to bed before five in the morning. It was at least 5:30 a.m. when I lay down, and we had to get up at 8:30 a.m. None of us got more than a couple hours of sleep. Everyone was tired on the flight home. There were people dragging on the plane, but it was the best dragging feeling ever.

—◆—

The dragging was even more extreme for Tyrel's family and his girlfriend, Jessica Menard.

The group was large enough that Stacy had reserved two rooms – one for men and one for women – and Stacy slept on the floor of their hotel room, on top of a bunch of Final Four seat cushions they had gotten at the Alamodome.

He had to take off work at Burlington (Kansas) High School to make the trip, of course. The championship game was on a Monday, and Stacy had to be back at school by Wednesday morning. So after celebrating at the team hotel for a few hours, Stacy made a proposal.

"I talked everybody into getting in the vehicle at three in the morning," Stacy said. "I drove us back. We drove into Burlington when the team was coming onto the football field in Lawrence. We watched it on TV."

—◆—

Whenever we fly, which is most of the time, we fly in and out of Forbes Field in Topeka. When we landed at Forbes that day, we got off the plane, walked into the terminal and saw this mass of people in there cheering. It's an older terminal, and there aren't a lot of flights going in and out of there anymore, so it was basically us and a whole bunch of fans. Coach Self stopped and said a few words and we all passed through some ropes, slapping hands with people. They were doing chants and cheering. You feel like a celebrity. It was an amazing feeling to know how much people care about Kansas basketball. It really does turn you into something of a celebrity in certain contexts. I never asked for that, and it's not the reason I started playing basketball, but it's an awesome feeling to be wanted. There is no greater feeling in life than when a kid asks you for your autograph or a parent wants to come up and say you have affected their child, and you're a role model. I was so fortunate to have experienced that.

We didn't stay at Forbes long. Maybe 10 minutes. If we stayed much longer, people would have started wanting autographs and pictures and it really would have taken a long time. Don't get me wrong, we love doing those things, but we had to keep moving.

From Forbes, we rode a bus back to Lawrence, where there was a gathering at the football stadium. It was a dreary day. Just rainy and cold and nasty. We had just come back from sunny San Antonio, so none of us was ready for that.

There was a huge outpouring of people. It was so awesome to see a football stadium filled with thousands of people who were there just to greet a basketball team that wasn't even playing anymore. I don't know how many places in the country something like that would happen, fans filling a football stadium just to welcome home a basketball team.

All of this, of course, happened on April 8, which is my birthday. I turned 19 that day. What a birthday present all of that was! The thing was, by the time we left the football stadium, I was so tired, I just went straight to bed for the rest of the day. I didn't even stop to eat. So there went my birthday.

Gone. I didn't end up celebrating my birthday nearly as much as the national championship, which was perfectly fine with me. I'll never forget that birthday.

Five days later, we had a parade through downtown Lawrence, which I heard had been pretty crazy the night we beat Memphis. That parade was kind of our way to experience that, even though you couldn't really describe the scene as "crazy" during the parade.

I had seen photos from the 1988 parade, and it was huge. That '88 team was an under-dog group and it had been 36 years since KU had won a championship. So there was a lot of pent-up emotion in

I didn't know what to expect as far as a turnout for the parade. I was blown away. It was a sea of people, just like we had seen in videos of the 1988 championship.

KU fans. We didn't know what to expect for ours. It wasn't that we were necessarily expected to win the title, but we had been a top-three team basically all season. It wasn't a surprise we made the Final Four.

But, man, the parade did not disappoint. The school estimated there were 80,000 people there. I rode in the back of a convertible with Matt Kleinmann. It was so cool. We were going slowly and people were right there. We could slap hands with them and spot faces in the crowd. It was a lot like our arrival at Forbes, but on a huge scale.

President Bush seemed like a normal guy. He was funny.
He also loved all the guys from Texas, like Chase and Darrell Arthur.

It doesn't really make us feel important, per se. When you think of it in the context of life, it's just a huge basketball game we won. But it did affect so many people and made so many people happy, it's really just an honor to be part of that team and bring so much joy to people's lives. It's crazy to think about that. It's just one win, but it can change your life with the doors and avenues it opens up for you the rest of your life.

Danny Manning knows a little something about that. He was the star of the team that won it in '88 and he was on the coaching staff at KU in 2008. In those minutes after the game, when we were in the locker room, Coach Manning came over to us freshmen and said, "You guys don't know how lucky you are, as freshmen, to do this." It didn't set in at that moment because you don't know any different. You're a freshman and you just won a national championship. You don't know the heartbreak that other teams have had and that you will have. You just think this happens every year.

Now that I look back on it, there might not have been a truer statement than that.

The "First" Tyrel

In a sense, Tyrel Reed is not the first "child" of Stacy and Debbie Reed to bear that name.

When they were in high school, Debbie was doing one of those home economics projects in which you care for a doll as if it were a real child. Stacy suggested she name it Tyrel, a name a young Stacy had taken a shine to in reading a series of western books by Louis L'Amour, some of which followed a family called the Sacketts.

"The youngest was called Tyrel," Stacy said. "He was considered the fastest gun in the west back then. They even made a movie out of it. I just loved that name from the moment I read that back then and I always said if I had a son, that was going to be his name."

And so it was.

"When he was born, the first question my mom had was, you didn't name him Tyrel, did you?" Debbie said.

So obsessed with Louis L'Amour's work was Stacy that he wanted to give his daughter a L'Amour character's name, too. The one he liked best was Echo.

"I put my foot down at Echo," Debbie says.

Lacie is forever grateful.

"Oh, so glad," she said. "I mean, oh my gosh. Even though my name is not Echo, but the fact my dad thought about calling me Echo. Like, Dad, you know how much people would have made fun of me?"

Don't let anyone look down on you because you are young, but set an example for the believers in speech, in conduct, in love, in faith, and in purity.

1 Timothy 4:12

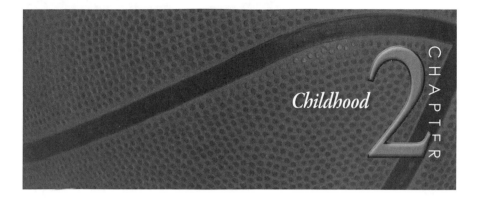

Childhood

CHAPTER 2

I am going to tell you something that happened during my childhood that is both partially boring and mystifyingly wacky. This event will explain a lot of things about the childhood I experienced and the kind of kid I was. It will also tell you something about The Benevolent and Protective Order of Elks.

So let's do this.

When I was in fourth grade, I entered a free-throw contest at the Elks club in Eureka, Kansas, where we lived. You know the Elks. It's like the Knights of Columbus or something. Or maybe it isn't. I don't really know much about it, except that it is a club of some kind and they have a building and they host a free-throw shooting competition for fourth graders.

Well, I won the local competition. After that was the Kansas state Elks free-throw shooting competition, and I won that, too. This meant I moved on to compete against winners from Colorado, Nebraska and, oddly, Wyoming. This competition was in Denver.

Now, at the time, I did not think anything about this was strange. But looking back, this was a pretty bizarre competition. Probably the strangest thing about it was that the Elks free-throw shooting competition was incredibly formal. Your performance was measured by 25 shots, but you did not simply step to the line and shoot 25 times. That might have been a little too simple. Rather, they lined all of us up in chairs arranged at mid-court. Boys shot on one end, and girls shot on the other (my sister, Lacie, had also made it to Denver). You would shoot 10 free throws, then go back to your chair and watch everybody else shoot 10 free throws. Fifteen minutes later, you went back up in the same order, having sat in a cold chair in a cold gym, and shot your final 15 foul shots with no warm-up attempts.

I must have been pretty pumped about something.

Looking back, this is a hilarious way of holding a free-throw competition. You could not get into a rhythm at all, and as far as I can tell there is no practical reason to do it this way. And I am not sure I could effectively shoot them this way today. But on that day in Denver, I made my first 10 shots, sat down for what felt like forever, then made 15 more shots. I made all 25 shots. The crazy thing was, some other kid had done the same thing. The Elks free-throw competition had become a shootout. We each got five more shots. The other kid made four, and I made five.

As far as the Elks were concerned, I was the best fourth-grade free-throw shooter that could be found between the Rocky Mountains and the Missouri River.

The Elks did not take this distinction lightly. The Elks – and I am still amazed at this – flew my family to Springfield, Massachusetts, to place me in the national Elks free-throw shooting competition.

I kind of wonder what happened to that poor kid who went 29-for-30 and didn't make it to nationals, but based on what I saw in Springfield, I'm not sure we should assume he went on to play college basketball or anything. This is because what I saw in Springfield astounded me. At some point in the trip, all the kids who made it there played in some kind of scrimmage and, I'm telling you, there were kids at this thing who could not even dribble.

I have to conclude there were kids out there who poured their entire basketball aptitude into shooting free throws, perhaps like the kids who compete in spelling bees. I can't imagine that, just shooting free throws all day. It must have been so boring.

The kid who won it made 24. I made 22 and got seventh.

I know I did not dream all this up because after a game at KU one time, a little kid came up to me and said he had heard I had done well in the Elks free-throw shooting competition. That little kid had made it to Denver. So I know this still exists.

You now know that I was the type of kid who competed in and won free-throw competitions held by fraternal orders.

If you learned nothing else from this, you now know that I was the type of kid who competed in and won free-throw competitions held by fraternal orders.

This is because I was the kind of kid who did pretty much everything he could fit into a day. I think I might have Attention Deficit Disorder pretty bad and I think it has always been that way.

As a kid, I was off the wall. I always had to be doing something. I was kind of annoying, probably. I'm that way to this day. I hate sitting in a house. My roommates I live with now say they'll be trying to watch a movie and I'll be surfing the Internet or walking around. I hate to be sitting still.

I get a lot of this from my dad. I have heard from a lot of people that he was an outstanding high school basketball player at Hoisington High School in Kansas. He ended up playing at Panhandle State in Goodwell, Oklahoma, but that was partially because an ankle surgery cost him most of his senior year in high school. If he hadn't gotten hurt, he possibly could have played at a Division I school.

That would be a horse's head attached to a stick. I still remember that thing. I wasn't real into toys, unless it was a ball of some kind.

I do not get this from my mom. The most athleticism I think my mom has ever displayed was making the ice cream cones at Dairy Queen when she was in high school. She and my dad were high school sweethearts. They got married soon after high school and eventually moved to Eureka, where Lacie and I were born. I was an easily scared kid. Such a mama's boy.

I got scared every day going to school. Was anybody going to pick me up? Was I just going to be left there? I would cry. In first grade, you start doing fire drills and tornado drills, and those terrified me. The alarm freaked me out. Every time it happened, I cried. They had to call my mom a couple of times because I would cry until somebody came to get me. You couldn't pry me away from my mom.

——◆——

I went as Dracula for Halloween once.

Lacie recalls one time in particular that Tyrel was pried away from his mom, and it did not go well.

"My parents went to Boston on a vacation, and it was our first time being away from our parents," she said. "We were at the airport and my brother is just bawling and bawling and bawling. He cried that whole day. He was sad my mom wasn't in reach, that she couldn't just pick him up and take him. I was trying to make him play with me and forget about it.

"At his senior day I was just thinking about funny things he and I have done together. That was one of the things that popped into my mind when he was giving his speech. That little boy that cried and cried and cried because he missed his mommy is now graduating from college and playing basketball and he's a role model for a lot of kids. Dang, he did come far."

——◆——

Whenever my family would take a vacation, like this one in Tampa,
I made sure I was going to be able to get some shots up during the trip.

I was really scared of the actual storms, too, which is a tough thing to be afraid of if you live in Kansas. Now I love them, but I was such a scaredy-cat back them.

Although I was extremely active, I think I was mostly a well-behaved kid. I did have one issue though: My mouth. I had a bad mouth until about my sophomore year in high school. I try not to cuss, now. I really do. When I became a Christian as a sophomore in high school, that was one of the things I wanted to eliminate from my life. It still happens from time to time, but I try. When I was a little kid, though, I'd always get my mouth washed out with vinegar. It was terrible. Some people used to get soap, but I would get vinegar. When my mom would use soap, I thought that was a treat. It was 10 times better than that vinegar.

When I got in trouble, either parent would dish out the discipline depending on who was there at the time. It's kind of a funny thing about my mom. She is the sweetest, kindest lady. She has such a kind heart. She never raises her voice. But then … I don't want to say she's got a little street in her, but she's tough. She would give us a smack, give us a spanking.

The worst trouble I ever got in was, of course, because of my mouth. I was in fifth grade. If you did something wrong, you would get a check mark. Well, I had gotten a mark early in the day. I called a kid a name. Then I got another mark for talking in the lunch line. Now, my teacher claims I said something back to her, but

What a sweet jersey, huh? I was in fourth grade in Eureka. You played flag football all season and at the end of the year, you played a tackle football game. As you can tell, it rained that day.

to this day I maintain I didn't say a word. I admit that I was talking, but I will not admit I talked back to Mrs. Powell, because I did not talk back to Mrs. Powell. My protests did nothing to change my destiny, however. There was going to be a note sent home to my parents. In fifth grade, about the worst thing you can do is get a note sent home to your parents.

My mom was pretty cool about it. She told me she was disappointed in me and instructed me to always obey my teachers. My dad spanked me when he got home. And that was that. My parents didn't dwell on things. You got in trouble, you got disciplined. Don't do it again.

Now, I wouldn't say this happened to me a lot. I was like most other kids. If I got around some people, I could get into trouble but I was a good kid at heart, I think. Just really energetic.

Lacie was still better than me at a lot of things when this photo was taken

What this meant for my childhood was that I was always running and jumping and playing one sport or another. I made my first "jump shots" on a Playschool hoop in the back yard of this tiny rental house where we lived in Eureka, Kansas. I was born in Eureka, where my dad was the basketball coach and government teacher and my mom was working on her teaching degree. My dad used to spend hours and hours out there with Lacie and me. When I got a little older, he put a terrible little basketball goal out front. When I shot on that goal I pretended I was Paul Pierce, the great KU player.

---- ◆ ----

Being Tyrel's father was a sometimes exhausting experience.
"There were days I'd come home dead tired from work and we
were doing something with a ball. He didn't have a whole lot of toys. He
never really wanted a bunch of different toys. He didn't play with cars or
tractors. But any ball he would play with. I would sit out there for hours
on end. We'd punt, kick, pass, shoot, baseball, soccer, anything with a
ball, he was playing. You had to keep him active. I think that has a lot to
do with the way he was able to spend so much time in the gym as he got
older. He was just that active.

"I'd come home a lot and he'd say let's go outside. I remember being
so tired I'd get a lawn chair out and sit by the basketball goal and teach
him stuff. He and his sister both. I remember teaching them one-ups.
That's how I would teach them right and left handed layups. I'd say one,
and then up. I'd make them take one step. I'd make him do so many on
the right and so many on the left. Everything he and I do, it seems like
we make it a competition."

—◆—

I have pictures of when I
could just barely walk and I've
got a basketball in my hands,
shooting. That was always the
sport I was best at, but it was far
from the only sport I competed in
as a kid. I would try anything. I
played baseball and football and
ran track and raced Lacie to see
who could finish our cereal first
or make it to the front seat of
the car.

My first real dunk wasn't until seventh grade,
but I started practicing early.

Lacie is 18 months older than me and was a really good athlete as a kid. She was always better than I was at everything until probably third or fourth grade. She would beat me in everything, and she would rub it in. Lacie is a lot like my dad. She's very competitive and fiery. She will get in your face if she needs to. And that just wasn't me. Honestly, personality-wise, I'm more like my mom than my dad. My mom is pretty calm, cool, collected. Fairly reserved on things. Doesn't yell at anyone. Just has the sweetest heart. I'm kind of the same way. It's hard for me to get really mad at somebody. And my dad and my sister are

Fishing has been a part of my life as long as basketball has.

the opposite. They'll get up in your face and do whatever they have to in order to get you going. I just can't do it. I'm too nice.

Sooner or later, I started taking after my dad a little more, at least when it came to competition. So eventually what we ended up with was my dad and my sister, a couple of really competitive, maybe even hot-tempered, people running around in there, plus me, a hyperactive kid who was always competing with my dad and my sister. I got into it with both of them at one point or another. It was always friendly competition, but everything my dad and I do is a competition. He hates losing to me in golf to this day. We've gotten pretty mad at each other over the years, but it all comes back to how we're wired.

Even when I was in college, every summer my dad and some of my friends and I go up to Colorado. (Inset) This is from one of our trips to Colorado

My mom was the glue of the whole thing.

And then you have my mom, behind the scenes, managing all this. She isn't all that competitive, but she was always there holding everything together. She grew up on a farm and worked hard her whole life. Our house was always clean, she was always making sure we got our chores done. Do this. Do that. But always with a kind, gentle heart. Lacie was in sports, I was in sports, my dad was coaching, but she was always kind of in the background. She was the glue of the whole thing.

In my college basketball career, you could see all of these elements of my personality come out. You can definitely be nice to a fault, and that has sometimes been true of me. Being with Coach Self and growing these past few years, I was able to be a leader and be more vocal.

Then again, there were some things I did in the heat of the moment during games that I think surprised some people.

One of the most memorable of these events came during a game at Oklahoma in 2009. Led by Blake Griffin, the Sooners were No. 3 in the nation at the time, though Griffin didn't play that night because of a concussion.

It was a game of gigantic swings. Oklahoma led by 14 midway through the first half, then Kansas led by 20 midway through the second half. With 3:40 left it was a three-point game again. Most people remember this as the game in which Sherron Collins made a three-pointer from nearly 30 feet out.

Just before halftime, Tyrel made a big three over Willie Warren, then turned around to let him hear about it.

Fans delighted in this, uploading the footage to YouTube and making .gif files of it to enjoy over and over.

That same season, after a mid-court scrap involving some Jayhawks (primarily Mario Little) and some Cornhuskers (primarily Cookie Miller) in a close game at Nebraska, Tyrel buried back-to-back threes and shouted something in Miller's direction after the second one.

"Tyrel got a little jaw-jacking in, a little out of character for him," Collins said afterward. "He keeps hitting big shot after big shot for us. He doesn't back down."

In his senior season, Tyrel hit a game-clinching three at Missouri, and turned to the Missouri student section to let out a roar. The photo of this moment also was a hit with KU fans.

The Jayhawks won all three of those games.

"I think he's so into the game, he really doesn't remember doing that," Stacy said. "He's just yelling. I laughed when he hit that big shot at Missouri and they showed the clip over and over. He's just screaming. He's not saying a word. I think people wondered what did he say. He's not saying anything."

These moments would cause Lacie's phone to blow up.

"I would get so many text messages from people like, 'What is up with your brother? I have never seen that side of him,'" Lacie said. "It's in there. It rarely comes out, but when it does it's the funniest thing ever. I loved it."

*People always ask me what I say when I'm yelling. Truthfully, I don't think
I ever say anything. It's just a yell.*

So did his teammates.

"I always laughed, I liked it," Aldrich said. "Tyrel was always competitive whether he said anything to anybody else on the court or not. It just created a little energy for all of us on the team because a guy who kind of keeps to himself on the court hit a big shot and talked a little crap. That lightens the team up a little bit. A lot of us were like, 'Damn, Tyrel's talking some crap? Wow.' You just laugh because Tyrel's such a nice, caring individual."

Debbie said she was just as surprised as anybody.

"It was so uncharacteristic," she said. "It was so out of character. We were like everybody else, saying what were you saying? He was like, 'I don't think I said anything, I just screamed.'"

Something about being on the floor brings out something inside him. "The only time he ever cusses is when he's on the basketball floor," Debbie said. "He says 'I don't know when I do it or why I do it.' I guess you get so excited you lose control a little bit."

—◆—

I think that's just the side that I have but I don't show. It comes out of the blue. I don't even know when I do that stuff, honestly. People are like, what did you say to him? I don't say anything. I just scream or yell. I'm so excited and caught up in the moment. That's the great thing about sports. It brings out the best in you. I'm not the type of player to yell and get in somebody's face. But I love to compete, regardless of how it's done.

I know that part of me is in there. I realize when I do it, but it's almost like you didn't really mean to, but you had to. You just hit a big shot. You've got to scream and get something out of there. I don't know.

Looking back on it, I think having an older sister who was (a) better than me and (b) bent on making sure that I knew she was played a huge role in making me the competitor I am today. I think it was good that she did that.

—◆—

Lacie's athletic advantage mostly had to do with her being 18 months older than Tyrel, which meant there was an inevitable moment coming.

"My dad kept telling me, 'Lacie, one day this isn't going to happen anymore,'" she said.

That day arrived when she was in third grade, when an argument turned into a wrestling match.

"I started punching him and wrestling around with him and all of the sudden it was like he was a different person," she said. "He pinned me. I ended up crying. I was like, 'Dad, why is he doing this?' My dad was like, 'I told you this day was going to come.'

"It's cool to be able to beat him and look back and think I was better than him at one point. It wasn't very long, that's for sure."

Stacy thinks getting beat by his sister helped form Tyrel's competitiveness.

"Lacie could outshoot him in layups when they were little," Stacy said. "The next thing you know, when the ball would be put up, he would run out there and get it again after she left and be working at it. He was so mad that he got beat."

Stacy never took it easy on his son, either, which sometimes infuriated the boy.

"He would get so mad at me for beating him," Stacy said. "I said, 'Son, do you want me to let you win? If you want me to let you win you're never going to get better. I want you to beat me when you can beat me and feel happy you were able to beat your dad.' I did the same thing to Lacie. Be happy you can beat somebody when they're doing their best. Nobody should ever want somebody to be given something."

The most traumatic of these instances occurred at a KU basketball camp when Tyrel was 6 or 7 years old.

"I worked with the Little Jayhawks for 25 years, and I brought Tyrel to camp for the first time," Stacy said. "We were playing knockout and we were playing a camp champion knockout. Ty had won so he got to go against the coaches. All the other coaches got knocked out. I wouldn't let that happen. I knocked him out in front of all the kid campers. He *was so mad. He cried. That was one of those times I gave him that talk. I said, 'Did you want me to let you win in front of all those guys or did you want me to let you win when you can and you beat me because you beat me when you were giving your best and I was giving my best?' I can still remember how mad he was at me.*

"That's the way I tried to bring him up. I didn't want to embarrass him, but if you beat somebody you want to beat them at their best. You don't want somebody to be hurt. You want to beat them at their best. That's the way it should be, or at least that's my feeling."

—◆—

I feel terrible for my sister because when she got to about sixth grade she started hurting her knees. She has dislocated one of her knees like 16 or 17 times. She's torn her MCL, torn her meniscus, had multiple surgeries. She continued playing basketball and multiple sports throughout it. I don't know how she did it. She's a lot tougher than I am. She just was a lot slower than she was when she was little. She was a great athlete.

—◆—

Lacie's first dislocation happened, go figure, trying to beat her brother at something.

"He was this big high jumper, and I was watching him and I was like, 'I can definitely do that,'" she said. "I wanted to do it because he can. Instead of jumping, I planted my leg, turned, and dislocated my knee. That started my knee saga."

That was in fifth grade.

"As I got older, the dislocations came more and more," she said. "I had 14 dislocations on my left knee and four on my right knee. I've done stuff with my MCL and meniscus. I've had two surgeries. My 13th or 14th dislocation, I was still in high school, and I knew it wasn't worth beating up my body like that. I wasn't a star like Tyrel. So I decided I'm going to go to college and hang up my shoes."

Lacie played high school basketball in a giant bandage.

"I always looked like the dumb basketball player," she said. "I always laugh at myself. When I was in high school I had the two huge, black knee braces, and I always had bad blisters so I had to tape my ankles. So I'm this short, 5'3" little thing and I have two knee braces that are taking up most of my leg and the remainder of my leg is covered in tape, so you can see maybe an inch of my calf."

Lacie remains an athlete, if not a basketball player. She is an avid runner and, like her brother, has an excellent jump shot, which she would sometimes use to show up KU basketball players after practices.

"I didn't have the speed or the height," she said. "But my dad perfected my shot. I'd tell those guys, 'I'm not worried about losing in a game with you guys. I can shoot with you.'"

— ◆ —

But then in about fourth grade I started to catch her. That was about the time my athletic ability really started to show for the first time. I was always active and athletic, but when you live in a small, rural town like Eureka, you don't necessarily know where you stand. Maybe you're the fastest kid in your school or whatever, but in towns like that it's not uncommon to go to school with the same group of kids from kindergarten through

Lacie and I competed at everything. I was a pitcher and a shortstop in baseball before I quit to focus on basketball.

high school. That happened with my high school basketball team at Burlington. The seniors on our team that won the state championship my freshman year had been playing with each other since they were kids. That's just how it is in towns like that.

But I think my dad wanted to make sure I knew there are a lot of other things in this world besides Burlington, Kansas, or Eureka, Kansas. He always wanted me to strive to be the best in everything I did. He would tell me if you're not practicing, somebody else is. He wanted me to compete with the best of the best and was always willing to take me wherever I needed to go in order to do that.

—◆—

"I think I did that with both of my kids," Stacy said. "I wanted to expose them to more than small towns. What I was trying to do was expose him athletically to all kinds of sports. Track was an easy one. I was a track coach. I knew track was something I could expose him to. He did pretty well at the local level. I really wanted him to see what it was like out there. I wanted him to know there were lots of good athletes. Everywhere you go there's somebody that's better than you. If you get beat you can go back and work on it or choose not to. If you really want to be good, you have to work at it.

"We were not going to take him to track nationals because of the money situation. You know, teachers don't make very much. In the summers I was usually doing some driver's ed trying to make a little extra money. I was able to find a very cheap flight for both of us. I had a buddy who lived in Norfolk, Virginia. That's where nationals were. We slept on the floor about four days, and we rented a car. It was a fairly cheap trip. Ty would tell you his dad is pretty tight with his money. I'm not into eating out and all that stuff. The first night we went out and bought a bunch of peanut butter and bologna. We ate basically right there at the house or in the car. We made it a cheap trip.

—◆—

XXXII AAU Junior Olympic Games
Hampton Roads, Virginia
1998

We went out to the Junior Olympics on a budget, and I'm grateful my dad made it happen.

When I was in second grade, I started going to AAU track meets and I was pretty good. The next year, I made the nationals in the high jump and the long jump. Nationals were in Norfolk, Virginia, and you have to understand that we did not have a lot of money. We weren't poor, but a couple of teachers' salaries don't make cross-country family trips easy on the pocketbook. My dad saved up enough money to fly us out there. We didn't even rent a hotel room, staying on a friend's couch instead. We played miniature golf in-between events, went to a movie and went to the beach. I thought I was on top of the world. I got second place in the long jump and was the national champion in the high jump. I still have my gold medal.

That might have been the first time I realized I could compete athletically with anybody, and from that point on, it was one thing or another like that. When I was in fifth and sixth grade, I competed in Punt, Pass & Kick and Pitch, Hit & Run. If you aren't familiar, these are skills competitions built around the basics of football and baseball.

I didn't like wrestling much, but I did it because my friends did it. I was fine at it. I lost three or four times, but I didn't enjoy it.

It's pretty simple. In Punt, Pass & Kick, you punt, you pass, and you kick and whoever punts the farthest, throws the farthest, and kicks it the longest is the winner. The concept is the same in Pitch, Hit & Run. You compete in your area, and if you win you get to compete at the big league stadium in your region. For me, of course, those destinations were Arrowhead Stadium and Kauffman Stadium in Kansas City.

I made it to Arrowhead to compete against kids from the surrounding states. I made it to that twice. I got second one time and third one time up there. I was pretty good at football when I was a little kid.

You got to go out during halftime at a Chiefs game and throw. That was really cool. In baseball, I made it to a Royals game at Kauffman Stadium. I think I got second in that competition, as well. I was a pretty good all-around athlete when I was a kid. Still to this day I feel like I'm pretty good at all the sports.

When you made it that far, you got free tickets to the Royals game that night. But, and this will tell you something about my ADD tendencies, I couldn't go because I was involved in like three other things that weekend. We went up to Kansas City on Saturday morning for the Pitch, Hit & Run, then drove back to Emporia and played two basketball games. Later that night there was a track meet in Emporia, in which I think I competed in seven events. It was a Hershey's track meet, and you could pay five or 10 dollars and get into any event you wanted. That's just the kind of sports I did as a little kid. I was a nut. I had to be on the go and was annoying everybody.

All those sports didn't leave a lot of time for leisure, and I would have had it no other way. The one leisurely thing I did was read, but in my case calling reading a "leisure" activity would miss the point pretty badly.

In Eureka, my school had something called AR, the Accelerated Reading program. I still have some records in Eureka for that. It worked like this: The more books you read, and the more challenging the books were, the more points you got. You'd have to take a test on it to make sure you actually read the books. If you got 300 points, you got to be the librarian for a day. If you got 500, you got to be principal for the day. Well, I really wanted to be principal for a day. I needed to be principal for a day. I would go home and read all night.

I got 500 points. I was principal for a day.

I was also big into Pizza Hut's Book It program. If you read a certain amount, you got a free personal pan pizza. I ate a lot of personal pan pizzas back then.

I still love reading to this day, although I don't do it enough.

I have never been able to just sit still and watch movies or sit

For some reason, I can sit there for hours and fish, but I can't sit still long enough to watch a movie.

around inside, but the one leisurely thing I have always loved is fishing. When I was a little kid, my dad would take me fishing and take me camping in various places around Eureka. Every summer up until now we've gone to Colorado and gone fishing the first week in June. I did that throughout college. Right before I'd get back to start Coach Self's camps, I'd go fishing. I love to do that to this day.

I used to go with all my high school friends. I had a core group of about six guys and four dads who would pack in a bunch of cars, stay in a tent, and fish for three days and come back. It kept building and building beyond fishing. We would go whitewater rafting or go golfing, which I still love.

What I have always loved about fishing is being in the outdoors. I love the serenity. Having no care in the world. You're throwing a lure out, reeling it in, and trying to catch a fish. There's nothing more manly or simple than that.

I think a good fisherman requires patience and perseverance. You're not going to catch a fish right at first. Especially in Colorado when you're trout fishing. You may catch one fish on your whole trip if you're lucky. On some of those trips some of my friends didn't catch a thing all weekend. I feel like I've got pretty good patience, which I learned from my parents. They were always so patient with me when I was running around, bouncing off the walls. I'm very fortunate. They instilled those good virtues in me.

We moved to Burlington when I was in sixth grade. My dad got a job at the high school there, but we hadn't sold our house in Eureka yet, so my dad, my sister, and I moved to Burlington the summer before my seventh grade year. My mom, who was a first grade teacher, stayed back in Eureka.

It was kind of a tough year not having your mom around, only seeing her on the weekends, not seeing her at your basketball games or football games. The next year, we sold our house and she got the eighth-grade science job. She was my eighth-grade science teacher. Maybe some people wouldn't want their mom as a teacher in junior high, but I enjoyed it. My friends were cool. They knew my mom and liked my mom. I was a pretty good student. I didn't cause too much trouble, so it was never a big thing.

The summer before that, I experienced a major athletic milestone. I had gone up to the school's gym, where some high school guys would go to play in the summers. They were all messing around trying to dunk. Some of them could. Well, I threw the ball up off the bounce and dunked it. I was kind of surprised. I was probably 5'8" or 5'9". From there, you know you can do it, so I kept doing it and doing it and doing it. That's how I got to be such a good jumper. I became obsessed with it. I would always try to do it at the end of practice. I would always stick around and try to dunk a hundred times.

— ◆ —

Despite Tyrel's prodigious leaping ability and all-around athletic conquests at a young age, Stacy wasn't ready to declare his kid a Division I prospect until the coaches started calling.

"In basketball, you've always got that kid in seventh grade who's bigger and stronger, and their mom and dad may think he's going to be the next LeBron James. I've seen it for years. I get a kick out of that because I don't know you can really say at that age a kid is going to get to that point. You'd have to really look at the skills first. Ty's skills were there, but Ty weighed 105 pounds in seventh grade and he was 5'7". I don't think you can say a kid's going to be a Division I athlete at that level.

He cautions against making projections on kids before they have physically matured.

"There are kids growing up you know are better than everybody in third, fourth, fifth grade because they're bigger and stronger, but you don't know how good they're going to be," he said. "I never put Tyrel in my mindset that he was a great athlete. I knew he was a good athlete. He was always as fast as anybody in town his age, and he could always jump as high, but I always thought, 'we're in a small town,' and I kept trying to make sure he's exposed to the outside. I think he said 'I'm going

to outwork everybody I'm around.' With basketball, I didn't know what level he was going to play at until after his freshman year in high school and he got his first offers from Division I schools. He could have gone to an Emporia State or a Washburn. To get your education paid for, every kid has those kinds of dreams."

—◆—

I got my first dunk in a game when I was a sophomore in high school. I don't know how many total dunks I had in high school, but I probably had 15 dunks my senior year. I dunked a lot. It was never one of those things I got immersed in, like I've got to dunk everything. There are definitely people who dunk once and suddenly that's all they want to do. They forget that's a pretty small part of the game and you don't get that opportunity very often.

I didn't dunk a whole lot at KU, which is to say I dunked exactly once in a college game.

Anybody who watched me in college knows that wasn't me. I didn't dunk a whole lot at KU, which is to say I dunked exactly once in a college game. I did it all the time in practice, and whenever we'd do testing I would always have the highest vertical on the team.

I'd say there were probably five or six times in my KU career when I had a chance to dunk and passed it up. A couple of those times I had expended myself so hard on the defensive end to get the steal that when I got to the rim I could barely touch the backboard. A couple of times I was just afraid of missing. In college your opportunities are pretty limited, and if you get an opportunity to play, you want to make the most of it. I'm not going to ruin my chances of playing by missing a dunk and not getting two points. I'd do it in practice. I had no problem doing it in practice, I just passed it up in the games.

One of the reasons I didn't dunk during games is that I was afraid of missing it.

My junior year in the Big 12 championship game against Kansas State, I got a runout. I was wide open and just laid it in. I don't know why. But then the next year in the Big 12 championship game against Texas, I got another runout. I was hurt by that point, playing on an injured foot. I don't know what it was, but I just decided to do it. That was my only dunk in college.

— ◆ —

There is good leaping ability, and then there is Tyrel Reed's leaping ability. His senior-year roommate, Curt Welter, a good high school basketball player in his own right, has seen Tyrel do some astounding things.

"The day of his wedding, we pulled into his apartment complex," Welter said. "I drive a Hummer H3. He was in Sperry's (casual shoes). He jumps

up on my hood. He takes one step and jumps up on my car. No problem. I looked at one of the groomsmen like, 'Oh my God, did you see that?' He just walks off like nothing happened. It's things like that. His balance, too. We go to the lake quite a bit. We bought a tube. Watching him on the tube, he can stand up on the tube and do whatever. His balance is not what you see in a normal human being. I think a lot of people underestimate how good of an athlete he really is."

— ◆ —

My teammates saw me dunk in practice a lot, and they were pretty excited to see me finally do it in a game.

This brings up an important point for me, which is that I feel really blessed in my life. God gave me this ability to jump and for some reason he made me 6'3". My dad says he is 5'10", but he has got to be 5'9". My mom is 5'5". My sister is 5'4", tops. My dad's father is probably 6'1", but I don't have a lot of height in my bloodlines. Yet here I am, 6'3" with some God-given jumping ability.

—◆—

"I'm the unlucky one," Lacie said. "We took a funny picture for his senior picture and for my wedding of us back to back, and he was towering over me. These two kids are from the same family... I had blonde highlights in my hair when I was in high school with the senior picture. He had dark hair, I had light hair; he was tall, I was short. It's just funny. People always say we look like two different people, then they look us in the face and say, 'You guys are like twins.'"

—◆—

I think I've been so blessed. I'm so blessed from the Lord, who gave me the talents and the work ethic. I give all the credit to the Lord. My dad instilled in me that if you want to be good at something you have to work hard at it. Whether that be reading when I was little, I wanted to be good at it, so I just read all the time. Whether it was track or basketball or whatever it was, I just went at it 100 percent. I hope to continue that for the rest of my life. I think this is true for everybody. The Lord wants us to succeed in life, and by working hard and having our focal point on Him, it makes it that much easier.

Jaydreaming

There is a popular piece of artwork floating around Kansas called "Jaydreaming." It is a painting of a little boy in a KU jersey sitting on the lawn in front of Allen Fieldhouse, presumably daydreaming about being a Jayhawk one day.

Debbie Reed now sees her son in that painting, even suggesting it as a name for the book you're reading. And there is some significance to it.

Years ago, when Stacy Reed was working camps for Roy Williams, one of the mothers brought in a bunch of small "Jaydreaming" prints for everybody. Greg Ostertag got one and didn't really know what he would do with it, so he gave it to Stacy. Stacy had Williams sign one to Lacie and one to Tyrel and brought them home.

Years later, during Tyrel's freshman season at Kansas, Debbie had one of these prints blown up and framed in Lawrence. Tyrel signed the bottom and gave it to his father for Christmas.

"I always thought that was a cool story," Debbie said, "because he actually did live out that dream."

Therefore do not worry about tomorrow, for tomorrow will worry about itself. Each day has enough trouble of its own.

Matthew 6:34

Recruiting

CHAPTER 3

There are a couple of things that, having been through them, give me perspective not everybody will agree with. It's just that if I were in control over the universe, I would try to make things different.

The first is when a player drags out his recruitment. I think that is happening more than it used to, and I would rather see it taken care of early, if possible. I understand it creates publicity, but not all publicity is good publicity.

The second thing is when guys de-commit. First of all, an oral commitment doesn't mean that much at all. You aren't genuinely committed to going anywhere until you sign a letter of intent, so some people put too much weight on the oral commitment. That said, I just feel like your word should mean something. If I had committed to a school, told them I was going to accept their scholarship, then I backed out of that, I would feel like I was quitting on them. I wouldn't feel right doing that to a university. My parents would never let me quit anything I started. I like when a player commits to a university and sticks with it. I feel like he's 100 percent bought into what they're doing there and it's going to be a much better fit.

I know I had some teammates whose recruitments went that way, but I know they had their reasons for it, and I'm just glad they became my teammates.

Actually, you would probably be surprised that we, as players, don't follow recruiting as closely as fans do. We know who our coaches are recruiting because they come on visits and we may hear something here or there, but any fan who follows recruiting would know way more about it than we do.

We aren't on the Internet reading up on KU's recruits. Once guys are on campus, we're definitely part of the recruiting process trying to sell Kansas as the place for them. But our main concern is to keep getting better with the team we have.

I committed to KU in the fall of my senior year in high school, and it was a dream come true. The recruiting process with Kansas had basically been a life-long experience. I had been going to Roy Williams' camps all my life. He had become a good family friend. My dad has worked KU basketball camps for the last 24 years, so I had always been exposed to KU, exposed to coaches, used to that whole world.

I was as big of a Kansas fan as anybody growing up, but I didn't get mad at Coach Williams when he left for North Carolina. I knew he was doing it for the betterment of his career and, like I said, he was a friend. I have always had the utmost respect for him.

I was 14 when he left Kansas, so I was still in the early stages of the recruiting process. But I had gotten my first recruiting letter in eighth grade. It came from Valparaiso, and I felt pretty cool when I got it. I have no idea how Valparaiso, which is in Indiana, would have heard about an eighth grader in Kansas. I wasn't even playing AAU basketball at that point. But somehow they did and they sent me a letter. It didn't really say much. It had my name on it, but otherwise was a form letter, I think. Keep working hard, we'll continue following your career. Mostly it was a letter with Valparaiso on it. In eighth grade, that's pretty cool.

It started to build some steam the next year, but what really exposed me was playing AAU basketball, which I started doing after my freshman year at Burlington. Before that, I had played MAYB ball, which is similar, but it's just a smaller thing. It's mostly around Kansas and the surrounding states. I played on the Topeka Jayhawks. Kyle Weems was on that team, too. He went to Highland Park in Topeka and later became the Missouri Valley Player of the year at Missouri State. After my freshman year, I had a tryout with KC Pump N Run, which is an Adidas-sponsored team coached by L.J. Goolsby. At the time, some of the older guys on the team were Leo Lyons, who played at Missouri. I guess his name was Leo Criswell at the time. Brady Morningstar was on the team. Casey Crawford, who played at Colorado, and Ryan Wedel, who played at Drake and Arkansas State were there, too.

It was a letter with Valparaiso on it. In eighth grade, that's pretty cool.

I went against some of those guys in the tryout and did well enough that they added me to the team. Pump N Run has a 15-and-under team now, but at the time all they had was 16-and-under and 17-and-under, so I played up a year.

Now, I was fortunate enough to play on a really well-organized, well-coached AAU team. We had practices. Our travel was always taken care of. We were trying to play basketball the right way. It was a team game and we were all just trying to win as many games as possible. Maybe that sounds obvious, but it really isn't the point for all AAU teams.

I would say the main point of AAU basketball is for players to get recruited. It's kind of sad, really, what it's all about. It's about getting recognized by coaches and finding a team that's going to be able to do that for you. L.J. Goolsby is a great person and a great coach.

We were doing it for the right reasons, to play well as a team. Some teams aren't out there for that. They're all about the individual. They want the individual to score a bunch of points and they don't care how the team does, but if he gets noticed by college coaches, that's all they care about.

So you'll get some guys putting up a bunch of numbers and not really caring about the outcome of the games. To some extent, this is understandable. You're playing three, four games in a day sometimes. The losses just don't hurt as much or for as long. It stings to lose in the moment, but when you've got another game in two hours, you just move on.

One of the ironies of AAU basketball is that it's not like you can fool a college basketball coach by getting yours. They know how to scout talent; they know what good basketball looks like. This is their job, and they're really good at it. Still, I think there's too many people out there that get bad advice or get the wrong person in their ear or get on a bad team where you're just worried about yourself. Who cares how your team does if you're doing well and scoring a lot and doing things that get you noticed? That's what's sad. You should play basketball to get better and have fun and enjoy it with your friends and your teammates. That's not the case sometimes.

—◆—

A high school basketball coach himself, Stacy said he initially was cynical about AAU ball. He remains so to some extent.

"Being from a small town, you're really concerned – is that coach trying to get something out of his players?" Stacy said. "I'll tell you what, that coach is one of the best men I've been around in my life. L.J. Goolsby is straight as an arrow. He told me up front, 'You're in charge of

his recruiting, I want to coach him. I want him to be a better player.'"

"At first I thought it was a necessary evil, but by the time we got done I felt like he made Tyrel better, he made all the kids better basketball players and human beings. I appreciate the experience he had because I watched other programs at that time. I could see why AAU ball sometimes gets the rap it gets. It is cut-throat out there. AAU coaches are going to tell you what you want to hear. L.J. was always honest throughout the process."

There is one thing about AAU ball that still confounds Stacy.

"A kid who shoots the ball 25 times and makes seven shots, I don't know how you tell me that kid is the greatest player," he said. "I do know the level of talent you get to see across the United States is what AAU ball does. That is what I think they're looking at. How do you recruit a kid who just made eight shots in a row one game and the next game he misses 10 shots in a row? I've seen it time and time again. I often just go, 'Wow, that's not who I would recruit,' but I'm also not on the chopping block with a job at that level."

—◆—

My team was always pretty good. When I got older, we had Travis Releford and Conner Teahan on it, plus Kyle Weems. We won the Super 64 Tournament in Las Vegas with those guys one year.

The crazy thing was, another year we made it to the Final Four of that tournament and we were scheduled to play the DC Assault, which had Michael Beasley and Nolan Smith on it. But somehow, our flight time was all messed up. We were booked on a flight that was scheduled to leave before the game even started. So we had to leave. We didn't even get to play them.

Because AAU ball is so recruiting-oriented, and because you play so many games, you pretty much cross paths with everybody at one point or another. Basically, anybody about my age who played college

basketball, I probably played against at some point. We played
Sherron's team one year, and he torched us. Of course, that wouldn't
have been the first time he did that to somebody. I played against Cole,
too. You kind of get to know these guys. Everybody sort of knows who
everybody else is.

There is kind of a sense that we're all headed to the same place –
college basketball – and we will probably run into each other again at
the next level. I wanted all my teammates to be the best players they
could be and go to the biggest college they could, and I think all my
teammates felt that way, too. There are a lot of players out there who
are wishing bad on each other. I think that's kind of a sad thing about
AAU basketball. Obviously, there are really good coaches around the
country who do a good job, but there are a lot of others who aren't in
it for the player. They're in it for more than that.

I do think AAU basketball is a good thing, overall. I don't know
if there's any other way players could get that much recognition and
coaches could be able to watch players that closely and that frequently
through the recruiting period in July. Without AAU basketball that
wouldn't be possible. But I think there should be more restrictions
on who can coach teams and who can be involved with players.
Too often, players get involved with the wrong group and the wrong
players. They don't know it at the time. We're all young kids. They
just get headed down the wrong path.

It never made me nervous, but you definitely notice when
Mike Krzyzewski is at one of your games, or Bill Self or Skip Prosser
or Roy Williams. I might get nervous talking to them, but playing
basketball was always so natural and normal for me.

My life changed in some major ways my sophomore year.
Basketballwise, it was when coaches really started recruiting me in
a serious way, but my life changed in a more important way that

year, too.

I became a Christian my sophomore year of high school. By that, I mean I was born again. Before that year, I had gone to church and been involved, but I really wasn't living for God. I wasn't completely bought in. There was a youth group that met every Wednesday night at a Baptist church in Burlington. My sister had been going to it, but I didn't really want to. I was so busy with basketball and just didn't want to do it. Well, she finally convinced me, and I fell in love. I loved growing closer to God. From there, it blossomed. I started going to another youth group on Sunday nights called MAGLIGHT (Men's Accountability Group Living In God's Holy Truth). For the rest of high school, when I got back from my workouts, I would go straight to youth group. I was saved my sophomore year. It completely changed my life around.

—◆—

"I got involved when we moved to Burlington," Lacie said. "I met a friend and they offered for me to go. I loved it. I knew Tyrel would probably like it. I wanted Tyrel to be a man of God. It took some convincing for him to go, but when he finally went, there was no turning back. I didn't want to be too pushy and turn him away from it, because sometimes being the bigger sister, I am pushy. I didn't want that to be something I pushed him to do. Over time I was able to encourage him and tell him how much fun I was having. Finally, he went. He loved it."

Early on, Lacie feared a bad experience would turn her brother off to the group. They had gone on a retreat where they were playing games at night. Tyrel got hit in the mouth with a Frisbee, knocking out one of his front teeth, eventually requiring a root canal and a false tooth.

"He didn't want to go to this youth group, he finally enjoyed it, then I was like, 'Dang it, he's not going to like it now,'" she said.

—◆—

Before that, I was just playing sports and doing other things for my own satisfaction. After that, everything became God-centered. I wanted to glorify Him with my actions.

The trigger was just realizing how unfulfilled my life was. I was doing well in sports and in school but something felt like it was missing. In my heart I knew I had been downplaying the importance God had in my life, that He is in control of everything and that He had blessed me with so much.

I was baptized in the Catholic Church and grew up in it. I love the Catholic Church. I just went a different route. I felt like I wasn't living the right way. I go to the Morningstar Church in Lawrence, now. It's a nondenominational church. I'm accepting of everybody, and I don't want to come off like I'm preaching or talking down to anybody here. At the same time, this is really important to me. I believe Jesus is my Lord and savior and the teachings of the Bible are the way we should live our lives. The thing I like about Morningstar Church is that it teaches from the Bible. Regardless of what people think, the Bible is full of all our truths. We study from that. I understand there are other religions, and I respect that, but God sent his one and only son to die on the cross for all of us. I believe that's where we should place our faith.

I believe faith in Jesus is the way to heaven. I want everybody on this earth to experience the joys God can give them on this earth. I pray everyone has Him in their lives, so we can enjoy all of his greatness in Heaven together.

After that summer, going into my sophomore year, recruiting really started to pick up. Coaches would come to Burlington to watch me work out at the high school.

I'm sure it was really inconvenient for them, but they would have to come to the gym at six in the morning, which is when I got there.

From seventh grade until I graduated from high school, my dad and I got up early every morning and went to the gym at the high school. He was a coach, so he had a key, and we could get in at any time. I could see the gym from our house, but we drove there anyway because my dad needed his car there in case he had to leave during the day. I always took the ride. I guess you could say I still had a little high school laziness in me.

My dad would go lift weights or run on the treadmill or whatever, and I would be in the gym shooting, almost always alone. And I loved it. I would turn on the sound system and listen to music. The time always flew by that way. I would work on my ball handling, work on my shooting. I would put myself through all these scenarios. Three-two-one-buzzer. I was pretty clutch in those situations because I could get as many chances as I wanted. You could tell yourself, "Oh, I really wasn't trying that time." We had a machine there that basically rebounds the ball for you and fires it back. You can imagine a kid that age would rather be sleeping, but I also wanted to get better. I was pretty much obsessed with getting better. And it really helped that my dad and I were both committed to it. He knew I was getting up and I knew he was getting up. Neither of us wanted to be the one who didn't get up. I missed one, maybe two days of that in my entire six years.

—◆—

Stacy misses those days.

"It was probably one of the most fun times I've ever had in my life," *he said. "Maybe that's why Tyrel and I remain so close. We did so much together that we kind of understand each other without saying anything. The morning sessions were great because he'd go do all this and turn his music on. I'd come in and say, 'Why don't you do this today?' We'd set up chairs. Even though you're doing it by yourself, you can do some things. We'd come up with little things we thought would be beneficial. I'd constantly peek in on him. I was either on the treadmill or the stepper.*

I'd lift a little bit. It was a very fun time for me."

That began in seventh grade, when Tyrel decided he wanted to dedicate himself more seriously to basketball. Stacy was careful to make sure his son understood one important distinction, which Stacy remembers delivering like so:

"Son, I'm going to give you some advice from your dad. Your dad wants you to play basketball. I don't know what level you're going to play at, whether you're going to just play high school basketball, but I want you to be the best you can possibly be if you're gonna put this kind of time into it. I'll come down. I'll wake you up, I'll go with you, I'll do all that stuff. But you have to want it more than I do. Because I love the game, but me wanting it for you doesn't do any good. You have to want it more than anybody else. I am not going to go down there and knock on your door and shake you and wake you up and make you come.

That's completely up to you. But I will walk down and say, 'Hey, are you ready to go?' If you don't want to go, that's fine, but you have to realize you have to want it more than anybody else. It's completely up to you as to how much you want it."

Turned out, Tyrel wanted it.

"I still have parents who ask me, 'What do we need to do to make our kid motivated?'" Debbie said. "I always tell them the same thing. We didn't do it. Yes, we supported him. But we never had to push him. He always pushed himself. Lacie was a great athlete, but you never once saw her hit the floor at six in the morning to go work out. You either have it or you don't."

Stacy loved every day of it.

"Those years went by way too fast for me," Stacy said. "I thoroughly enjoyed and loved it and truly miss it, but Tyrel is moving on to another phase and I'm excited for the next phase, just like I am for my daughter."

—◆—

I really didn't mind being by myself. I love it being just me, the ball and the gym, shooting and rebounding for myself. It's therapeutic. The other thing was, if I was going to do this, the mornings were simply my best chance to do it. For three years of high school, I drove to Lawrence three days a week to work out with a trainer. That drive took an hour and 10 minutes. Before I had my driver's license, my mom would take me up there in our van. When I turned 16, I started taking my sister's Chevy Malibu. There was a lot of therapy in those drives, too. My life was so much going, going and going. That was a time I could have some thoughts to myself, listen to some music, whatever.

I can't even tell you how many times I have made the drive between Burlington and Lawrence. I went up for those workouts, and I went up to play pickup games with the KU players, too. I started doing that my freshman year. Since my dad knew all the coaches, they would just let me know when the guys were scrimmaging and I'd show up. It was really intimidating at first. Wayne Simien still gives me a hard time about that. They'd be playing and 14-year-old me would be on the sideline hanging out. They would ask me to play and I'd go, "Naw, I'll get the next one." I mean, these guys were heroes to me at the time. And they were bigger, stronger, and faster.

When I did get out there, I couldn't hang with them physically, of course, but I was always a good shooter. I held my own, and quickly realized they are people just like me.

Anyway, the point of all this is that I did not have a lot of extra time. If a coach wanted to talk to me on the phone, we would set that up in the evenings after I got back from Lawrence. But if they wanted to see me work out, that had to be bright and early.

I realize this schedule might seem kind of insane, but I really didn't know any different. I would have had it no other way. There is no way you could do all this in college. It would be too much wear and tear on your body. But in high school, you can handle that stuff.

Although I did gladly choose to do all of that, it was a sacrifice. For one thing, I had to sacrifice football, which I loved. I had been a lanky running back in junior high and probably would have been a quarterback in high school. But I decided my future was in basketball and that meant a full commitment. It also was a social sacrifice. Any high school kid wants to hang out with his boys, play video games, do whatever high school kids do. It wasn't that I couldn't do any of that stuff. I still had my evenings, but I had priorities and goals and I was going to do whatever I could to be as good a basketball player as possible.

Fortunately, I didn't have a cell phone until I was 17. I say fortunately because not having a cell phone meant college coaches couldn't call and text my cell phone all the time. My parents were really good about managing all of that, because the calls started coming in pretty much every day when I was in high school.

The conversations with coaches really aren't much. It's a lot of small talk. How's the family? How is school going? That kind of thing. They're really just trying to get a feel for you. That's one thing college coaches are really good at. They're salesmen. It's basically in the job description. You need to be able to do that to be an assistant coach or a head coach in college sports. I don't know if slick is the right word, exactly, but you've got to have a way with people that makes that family and that player feel comfortable with you. I think there are some college coaches that are great with people and maybe not as good with Xs and Os. They're just good with people. They're good recruiters and, I guess, good coaches, but mainly just good recruiters.

You probably can't be a head coach in college basketball without having some ability to make people feel good or make them feel special. Coach Self has that uncanny ability to command your attention and make you feel like you're the most important person in the room while he's talking to you. He may only talk to you for 30 seconds, but for that 30 seconds you feel like he knows you. Coach Self, once he meets you, will never forget you. He will remember your name for life. It seems like he knows everyone's name, regardless if they're your mom, your dad, your girlfriend, your brother's friend.

That's one of the things that makes him special.

I don't remember when I met him for the first time, but it would have been soon after he took the job at Kansas. I was too young to have known anything about his time at Oral Roberts and Tulsa, but I had known his Illinois teams and, as a fan, felt really good about him being KU's coach. I had a lot of respect for him.

You might think a Kansas fan like I was would have wanted to go to Kansas no matter who the coach was, but when you're a player, the specific coach is a really, really big factor. I wouldn't have gone to KU to play for just anybody. I had multiple scholarship offers by the time it was all said and done, including one from my friend, Coach Williams, at North Carolina. I had taken an official visit to Stanford and loved it. I could have gone there. Oklahoma offered me a scholarship. So did Missouri. I was blessed to have so many options.

—◆—

One option, in particular, would have caused a bit of a stir. Missouri coach Mike Anderson had one scholarship available in the 2007 class. Not only did he offer it to Tyrel, he told Tyrel he wasn't recruiting anybody else in that class. If Tyrel didn't accept it, Missouri wouldn't be signing anybody until the spring.

Anderson kept that promise.

"Little things like that stick out in your mind," Stacy said. "There is a coach that has guaranteed you he wants you. Some coaches do that and some others are always recruiting and you don't know where you are.

"He felt real bad telling Coach Anderson no."

The scholarship Tyrel turned down ended up going to forward Justin Safford, a Rivals.com three-star prospect from North Carolina whose best season was 2009-10, when he averaged 8.6 points and 4.1 rebounds.

Regardless of how much you love Kansas and the program and everything it stands for, which I had loved since I started watching basketball, you still have to take the coach into consideration. Believe it or not, whether the tradition is great or not, the coach in front of you is the one in charge of your playing time, not the fans or anybody else. That's a big consideration. You're going to be spending 80 percent of your time with these people. I loved Coach Williams when he was here and I loved him when he was at North Carolina recruiting me. When Coach Self took over, it was another great thing.

As a player, you still want to do your homework to some extent and get a feel for the coaches. Playing AAU ball helps. Your coaches have gotten to know other coaches. Other players have gone to various schools and you kind of hear what these guys are like, how they treat you, if they're honest. When you go on your visits, you talk to the players and ask a bunch of questions. What would coach do if this happened? Do you like your coach?

I think players are candid in those situations. I really do. At Kansas we were always honest with recruits whenever they asked us a question. I think that's just the code of honor you take. Most guys are not going to sell you something it's not, because we've been there before. We wouldn't want somebody telling us something that's not true. We were all being recruited at one time and we wanted to be told the truth, so we might as well tell them everything we know.

So, basically, Kansas was recruiting me all along, but not as aggressively as some of the other schools. I think the coaches sort of knew I liked Kansas and I was just down the road. I also think there is a stigma about small-town Kansas kids. I don't want to say Kansas Class 3A basketball isn't good competition, because it is. However, AAU basketball was a different level of competition. Playing AAU ball gave me the opportunity to compare myself to the best players nationwide, which is what coaches want to see.

————◆————

"Coach Self always told me he wanted Ty," Stacy said. "But there were a lot of coaches who said that. I think he was a kid that Coach really wanted and liked, but I think it came down to whether he should pull the trigger on a small-town kid. I think he watched him enough in AAU basketball that it finally brought Coach Self to the point he knew this kid could help his team.

"I don't know what necessarily was in Coach Self's mind, but I think that was always something that would play a little role in how you recruit a small-town kid. How is he going to adapt to the big school? How is he going to adapt to 16,000 people in Allen Fieldhouse or at Missouri? How's a kid going to do there when he hasn't been in that position?"

I was about 5'11" and 140 pounds my freshman year in the state tournament. I grew an inch every year of high school.

There was a moment in an AAU game that sold Self on Tyrel. Pump N Run was in the championship game in Las Vegas, and Tyrel bit his tongue all the way through so there was a hole in his tongue.

"He had blood coming everywhere," Stacy said. "There's nothing you can really do to a tongue. You could see a hole all the way through it. He was spitting out blood. He went over and grabbed a towel during a game. He didn't want to come out. He got all the blood out and swallowed it, threw the towel back down on the ground and played the rest of the game. Coach Self said, 'That's my kind of toughness.'

"I think Coach Self knew Tyrel had a love for KU and all he had to do was make an offer. Maybe he thought he could go out and get a better player than him. I don't know the process."
Self said he remembered that incident.
"It just meant so much to him," Self said. "That's the thing. Last year I went around and polled everybody: Who is the toughest kid on our team? It was totally unanimous, Morningstar and Reed were voted by their peers as the two toughest guys on our team. Certainly that was an indication back when he was young that it was mind over matter with him. He wasn't going to let anything like that hold him back."

—◆—

I always wanted to impress these coaches. Not every player feels like he needs to. Some players have more leverage in recruiting than most. I didn't feel that way. I always wanted to impress whoever it was watching me or recruiting me. That's just the type of person I am. I want to show people I belong and I am a good player. I didn't feel like I was entitled to any of this.

I'm not saying guys like Kevin Durant and Michael Beasley shut it down or whatever, but the experience of being one of the top two or three recruits in the country is a little bit different from my experience.

For guys like that, it's pretty obvious how the recruiting rankings work. I mean, LeBron James was obviously the best player in his class. But these recruiting sites like Rivals.com and Scout.com will rank at least 150 players, and I really have no idea how they evaluate it. I guess they see all of us play in various tournaments, but I don't know if there is some kind of metric they use or what. I know that at one point, I was ranked right up next to Marcus and Markieff Morris, so I guess that shows it is an inexact science.

Cole Aldrich obviously enjoyed college. He made the Jolly Green Giant costume himself out of felt pieces he bought. I, on the other hand, am not a big fan of Halloween.

I think it's great those Web sites exist. It's good for fans to be able to track that stuff and get to know their recruits a little bit before we get on campus. And I really did enjoy the attention. It was cool to have reporters calling and talking basketball with me, asking me what I thought about different schools. It can really help a small-town kid like me get his name out there.

Someone from Rivals or Scout would call me probably once every couple of weeks. It's different for different players, though. Somebody like Josh Selby, the No. 1 player in his class, was probably hearing from somebody every day. It would get busier in the summer, during the AAU season. If you were playing well, they would want to talk to you about that. If you weren't, they'd want to know why. They also ask about which schools you're considering. I know if you go to my Rivals.com profile, it will say I had offers from Kansas, Oklahoma, Missouri, Missouri State, and Stanford. That's all true, but I don't know how they decided to list those five. I had other scholarship offers, and when it came down to it, the ones I was most serious about were KU, Stanford, and North Carolina.

This is not to say I didn't give consideration to those other schools. I took an unofficial visit to Oklahoma the same weekend Blake Griffin was taking his official visit. I really liked Jeff Capel, who was the coach at the time. He was young and energetic. You could tell he knew a lot about the game from having played under Coach K at Duke. The only other school I officially visited was Stanford, and I loved that, too. Palo Alto (California) was beautiful. I liked Trent Johnson, who was the coach then. They had the Lopez twins, too, and I thought it would be fun to play with them. Obviously, the academic reputation was attractive as well.

Official visits, by the way, are awesome. The school is allowed to fly you and someone else out to campus. They kind of wine and dine you, put you up in a really nice hotel with your own room, take you to really nice restaurants. You might play some pickup ball with the guys on the team, have a meeting with the coach. At night, the guys will take you out. When I visited Stanford, we went to this big sorority party. We just hung out. Nothing was really going on, but it was just fun being with the guys. Maybe you go to the movies, just act like a college kid for a while. It's fun. You're in high school hanging out with a bunch of college kids, seeing what they do, seeing how they act. You're learning how to be a college guy.

In high school you're sheltered from everything. You're not very autonomous. Your parents influence all your decisions. When you go up there, you see things like, "Gosh, this guy's apartment is a mess, but guess what, he's on his own and he can do what he wants." That's awesome. Personally, I can't stand if something's messy. But you get the point. It opens your eyes to how much fun it is being on your own. That's why people say it's the best four years of their life. It really can be.

The idea of being on my own did appeal to me. I was not bent on staying near home at all. I love small towns. They're familiar and you have all your friends and it's great. But I was, and still am, interested in getting out and seeing the world. I'm not a homebody. I don't think I'll live in a small town again. I would have loved moving to California or North Carolina, and my parents would have been fine with that, too. They never pressured me to stay close to home. I always knew it was my decision to make.

There also were opportunities to go to any number of other smaller-name schools. I was interested in Missouri State because I had a lot of connections there. Ben Miller, who had been an assistant coach at KU under Coach Williams and is one of my dad's best friends, was an assistant at Missouri State under Barry Hinson. So was Steve Woodberry, who played at KU in the 1990s, and helped coach KC Pump N Run for a while. It did occur to me that I could go to a mid-major school and possibly be a star, something anybody would like. Who wouldn't want to be the go-to guy?

At some of the smaller colleges, the ones that weren't the Kansases, the North Carolinas, there may have been more playing time, but at the same time, I'm not afraid of taking on a challenge and trying to compete and show people I can do it. That never discouraged me from going to a bigger college.

I love to win. Going to a small school and being a star would have been cool, but I wanted to win a national championship and I didn't think going to a smaller school would have given me the best chance of doing that.

Playing time was a big part of it, too. Coach Self was pretty honest with me. He said they had a deep team with a lot of established guys at that point, and if I was going to play, I was going to have to beat out those guys, but that he thought later in my career I could be a big part of the rotation. That didn't bother me. I trusted him, and I believed I was good enough to contribute anywhere in the country if I worked at it.

—◆—

Stacy was playing both father and coach at this point.

"I had to give him every opportunity for coaches to talk to him and see him, but I also don't think a kid ought to grow up every single day having to get a call from a coach and being concerned about where he was going every second of his high school career. I wanted him to enjoy his life. I wanted him to enjoy his friends, enjoy school. I looked at it from two different viewpoints.

"I tried to manage it so he felt like he was getting a good feel for the coaches interested in him and the schools interested in him, but I also wanted to make sure he was able to go to his buddy's house and horse around on a Friday night if he wanted to."

The other thing Stacy wanted to manage was his son's expectations. "I knew if he got to the age, 16, 17, 18, he needed to figure out which school he wanted to go to. I knew there was that dream of being a Kansas Jayhawk. I also tried to make sure he knew that may not be an option. He needed to prepare himself to look at any school interested in him and give them the opportunity to recruit him. As a kid, the recruiting thing was like, 'Hey, I'm good enough, I'll go to Kansas.' You may be a good enough basketball player, but that may not be what they need in that recruiting class. So I had to explain to him, 'You could be good enough, but they might not need you in that particular year, so that's not where you're going to get to go. It could be they don't need somebody at that position or they could be recruiting five and you might be the third one.' I tried to give him the explanation of what the recruiting process was going to be like."

—◆—

I think all the coaches who recruited me caught on to this mindset of mine. Everywhere I went, I got a pretty similar pitch. No one ever just guaranteed me a starting spot. (Even if they say it's guaranteed, it isn't.) But I think coaches are good at knowing the player they're recruiting. They knew I was the type of kid who wanted to work hard and work for everything I got. It was always very "If you work hard and the chips fall into place, we could see you starting your freshman year. If not, we could see you being an integral part the years after that."

I wanted to be finished with recruiting during the fall signing period of my senior year. I never got all that close to committing anywhere else before KU offered. North Carolina offered a scholarship, but the way it worked out I was going to have to wait until the spring to accept it. I just didn't want to do that.

Suddenly, one day after school Coach Self called and said they had a scholarship available for me if I wanted it. I accepted it on the spot.

— ◆ —

Self said seeing Tyrel play against AAU ball was a part of the recruiting process, but it wasn't the deciding factor.

"Obviously, I wanted to see him play against AAU competition, but that wasn't what really sold me," Self said. "What sold me is just how hard he worked and how well he shot it. I thought he could become a great shooter, which he did."

Tyrel's family was, of course, thrilled with the decision, though nobody was happier than Lacie, who was already a freshman at Kansas and secretly hoping her brother would join her.

"From the time I was little we were inseparable," she said. "The year I was in college was pretty hard. We had gone from doing everything together, me being his biggest fan, to me being in college. I'm still coming home for his games and things, but in the back of my mind those 17, 18 years could have been it. That was hard for me to grasp. I would love for him to come to KU and continue to have that bond and watch him develop into a young man and become a better basketball player, a role model for kids. It was something really important to me. I never made that known, because it's his life and I wanted him to do what's best for him, but I always wanted him to come to KU."

She drove home from Lawrence to be there when he signed his letter of intent.

— ◆ —

Although I did not officially become a Jayhawk in that moment – I was not wearing the jersey – I still suddenly felt like I had to represent Kansas. The reason is that, before then, I was just a really good high school player. After that, I was suddenly an enemy to a great number of the people who were at my high school games. The road trips in 3A basketball take you to a lot of rural communities, and those rural communities tend to be more heavily populated by K-State fans, mainly because it is an agricultural school.

I mean, people are booing me everywhere we go, and it's not just that they are booing Burlington; they're booing me. And they're doing it because I chose to go to a college they don't like. It was kind of funny seeing people who are such K-Staters they can't even feel good for you going to Kansas. You don't know me personally, you don't know anything about me, yet you still hate me. I haven't showed any bad sportsmanship. I haven't done anything to any of your teammates or players who go to your school, but you hate me. It makes me laugh. My teammates seemed to enjoy this even more than I did, and some of them were K-State fans.

Opposing players seemed to like to get their shots in, too. Some guys would talk to me all game. It's like they're trying to take you down a peg. They're trying to take something away from you. You make a turnover or something and suddenly you're not good enough to be going to Kansas. Or some kid blocks your shot. It doesn't really matter to you, but maybe to someone else it's a big deal to block the shot of someone who's going to Kansas. Honestly, it was kind of fun. I loved hearing all that.

—◆—

"People from other communities at that time want a kid to fail," Stacy said. *"If he doesn't make a shot, he's really not that good. If he misses two or three shots, it's, 'Well, I'm as good as he is.' That's what you would get. There were communities that booed. I don't know why. That's probably something I'll never be able to explain.*

"I do understand the bull's eye. If that kid's got a KU scholarship, I want to guard him, I want to do everything I can to make myself have an opportunity. If a college coach was there watching you and Lon Kruger is sitting in the stands at Neodesha and I'm guarding Tyrel and I make 10 shots, maybe Lon Kruger is saying maybe we're not recruiting the right kid."

Stacy doesn't think it ever affected Tyrel.

"He had such a good core of buddies," Stacy said. *"If he had ever gotten cocky, those four or five guys would have brought him down really quickly, along with a dad who would have brought him down really quickly. I think his friends were really good. I think that helped a lot."*

—◆—

In a lot of ways, it prepared me for college. I developed a thicker skin and you need it. In college, rival fans are a lot more creative and a lot more bold with the stuff they'll come up with, the signs they'll make, things they learn about you somehow. I tried to keep my name out of the media, so I didn't get it quite as much as some of my teammates did, but still, when you play at Kansas, you live with a bull's eye on your back. In a small way, signing in the fall prepared me for that.

April 8, 2009

Dear Tyrel,

We really enjoy watching your game. You guys are the best team ever. I even know your chant, "Rock Chalk Jayhawk K.U." that's the chant. All of you are good players you all should be able to touch the ball. I really like your team even though you didn't make it to the finals. I'm looking forward to watching you play next year.

Your fan,
Alex

So do not fear, for I am
with you; do not be
dismayed, for I am your
God. I will strengthen
you and help you;
I will uphold you with my
righteous right hand.

Isaiah 41:10

Freshman Year

CHAPTER 4

There are rules. That's just life. Wherever you go, there are rules, some of which you might not even know about. Some rules you just have to learn by experience.

I am going to tell you about the time Cole Aldrich learned a rule this way.

Our coaches suggest that incoming freshmen arrive on campus the summer before your freshman year begins. It isn't necessarily required, but there are a lot of benefits to this. You meet your teammates. You play pick-up games. You work at Coach Self's camps. And you enroll in summer classes. I graduated from high school May 18 and was on campus June 2, ready to go to school.

This was the case for all the guys in that freshman class, which comprised Cole, Conner Teahan, Chase Buford, and me. We were enrolled in three credit hours for both of the summer sessions. Cole and I were roommates.

On the very first day of classes, Cole and I were walking to our sociology class. Cole was wearing jean shorts and a wife beater. (I would call this an A-shirt, which is the proper name, but I don't think anybody would know what I was talking about). In order to appreciate the rest of this story, you'll have to momentarily divorce yourself from the comic nature of (a) jean shorts and (b) Cole Aldrich in jean shorts.

It was Cole's misfortune that Coach Self just happened to be driving through campus as we were walking to class. He stopped, and the glass in his window buzzed down into the door. He leaned out and said, "Cole, what are you doing? You can't dress like that. We don't do that at Kansas."

He wasn't talking about the shorts.

And that's how Cole learned one of our rules. We aren't allowed to wear wife beaters in public.

Probably a lot of people wouldn't want to go to summer school, but I'm glad I did. The summer classes allowed me to graduate in three-and-a-half years, and it allowed me to work Coach Self's camps.

Late Night is an exception to some rules, namely the wife-beaters-in-public one.

Those are really your first events as a Kansas basketball player.

One of the things that is new for most of us is that these little kids come and ask for your autograph, which is great. But this is always a fun time for upper classmen, who get a kick out of watching the freshmen sign things. We're not experienced at it, so we're slower and our signatures usually need work.

My signature has always looked pretty good, because I'm fairly meticulous about my handwriting. So much so that it looks like a woman's writing. What can I say? I learned it from my mom. But because of this I was a little slow as a freshman. This probably isn't something most people think about, but we players pay attention to each other's signatures.

This might be because we spend so much time writing them. If I had to guess, I would estimate I have signed somewhere around 50,000 autographs in my life, and I'd like to think I have my signature down. It looks fairly decent, I can do it as quickly as anybody else, and even if you had no idea who I was, I think you'd be able to read it. When someone asks for my autograph it's the best feeling ever. I'd gladly sign until my hand falls off.

But there have been some pretty shaky signatures over the years. Cole has one of the ugliest signatures known to man. It's just a big scribble. This might be because he has probably signed a million more than I have. I don't know. Josh Selby had a pretty terrible signature. Elijah Johnson's was pretty bad when he was a freshman. They just need some more time to perfect their craft.

I've always thought Brady Morningstar had a great signature. He would write the "Morning" part, then sign a star. That was pretty sick. Sherron Collins has a great signature. The Morris twins have good ones. It just takes time, and upper classmen like to give the younger guys a hard time about it.

When my classmates and I were seniors at Late Night, we got to be a little less embarrassed than the underclassmen.

When someone asks for my autograph it's the best feeling ever. I'd gladly sign until my hand falls off.

The other thing that happens at those summer camps is the scrimmages. Believe it or not, these summer scrimmages will attract hundreds and hundreds of spectators. Usually there are some former players there, maybe some NBA guys or whoever. Guys like Scot Pollard, Greg Ostertag, Aaron Miles, Julian Wright. Whoever wants to be there. The current guys and the old guys will play in these pickup games. It's fun, but it's also nerve-racking for a freshman. It's the first time the fans and media can see you play as a KU player.

In that week or so of summer break I got between high school graduation and moving to Lawrence, I had all those nervous feelings you might think. Am I ready for this? I don't know, but here goes.

Once the actual fall semester begins, you have a few weeks to prepare for one of the truly terrifying experiences of being a freshman at Kansas: boot camp.

Boot camp is not very fun, which is the whole point. This is a two-week event specifically designed to make you miserable. The whole idea behind it is to put the team through a difficult time we all experience together, to break us down and then put us back together as a group of people who had to fight through something together. In other words, boot camp is the perfect name for it.

If I had to describe it in one word, I would use "excruciating," but fortunately I can use many additional words.

Here is the basic workout menu, from which you select *everything:*

1. Stretch and ladder drills.

2. Jump rope for three minutes, right foot, left foot, two feet. You run a sprint for every miss that the whole team has, which could be anywhere from 10 to 30.

3. Everyone then grabs a line and jumps over it front to back, then side to side, then in a box shape two minutes, with their hands above their heads.

4. Line up for defensive slides with Coach Self at the helm, telling us slide right, left, at an angle, take a charge, etc. You do this for five minutes or so. Then he will tell us to hold our stance til our legs shake and he begins to smile.

5. Then we go into stations. Each station is about two minutes long. There are four of them with no break. We will go through them each once or twice depending on Coach Self's mood. This will take between eight and 16 minutes.

- **Station 1:** Lane slides 30 seconds on, 30 seconds off. Each person goes twice or for a total of a minute.
- **Station 2:** Shell spots, which is where we practice being in the right position defensively on the court, being in passing lanes, etc.
- **Station 3:** Rim touches for 30 seconds on, then 30 seconds off twice. You touch the rim then back pedal to the free throw line and touch and then go back to the rim.
- **Station 4:** Closeouts for 30 seconds on then 30 seconds off, twice. You run and closeout at a coach then run back.
- Lastly, we run sprints every day, starting with maybe five or seven the first day and continue to build each day.
- The second-to-last day we run 20 of the sprints we call 22s – down, back, down and back again in 22 seconds. If someone misses a time or a line you don't count that sprint.
- The last day we do 30 suicides. You have 30 seconds to touch half court, 3/4 court, full court and back. You miss it, the whole team goes again.

Here I am, clapping in between pushups. Our strength and conditioning coach, Andrea Hudy, comes up with lots of creative ways to keep us in shape.

You have to be on the floor, dressed, taped and ready to run by 6 a.m., so Cole and I would get up about 45 minutes before that. You have to walk over from Jayhawker Towers, which is only a couple of blocks, but by October it's starting to get cold out, and it's dark and you're tired and all of that makes that walk pretty unpleasant.

We do the defensive stance drill for a minute, or what Coach Self claims is a minute. It feels like 10. And he isn't wearing a watch while he does it. After probably two minutes of this, your legs start shaking. I think that's actually how he decides when the "60 seconds" are up, when people start collapsing.

And that's at the beginning of the morning.

Boot camp really all builds up to the last two days. It's a two-week deal and you get the weekends off, but it's not like you can really take them "off," the way most people think of taking time off. Granted, you're not going to be working out, but you're not going to be going out, either. I don't drink alcohol anyway, but you don't want to be going out drinking or eating a bunch of junk. When you're working so hard that you need every last drop of energy and performance, little stuff like that can make a difference.

My one vice is pop. I drink way too much of it, and I know this. I don't drink coffee, either, so sometimes that's where I get my caffeine, but I can't really claim that as the reason. I just like the taste. My teammates would always make fun of me about this, but I figured that since I didn't drink alcohol I may have some leeway there.

But this does bring up an important point about boot camp. If you have not kept yourself in shape in the offseason, it is going to go badly for you unless you're a freak. It's simply too difficult.

In this context, you may wonder about Sherron Collins. It was pretty well publicized that Sherron tended to put on weight in the offseason every year. Usually he would come back from break a little overweight. Coach Self would get on him for that, and it always became a story in the media. I actually think Sherron probably took more grief for that than he deserved. I felt bad for him, because it wasn't totally his fault. He just has a body type that wants to add weight. He looks like a running back and in my eyes would have succeeded in that just the same way he did basketball. It was a deal where he could be eating the right things and still gain weight. He just didn't have as high of a metabolism to keep it off like some of the other guys.

"The crazy thing was, I don't know where he put that weight. Even if he was a few pounds up, he still had a six-pack, he still had the chiseled arms, and he could still get through all the running at boot camp. He just wasn't in nearly the shape he wanted to be in or Coach Self wanted him to be in. His body was really a blessing and a curse. It was his strength, but also maybe a weakness."

Sherron was a good enough athlete to make it through even when he wasn't in his best shape, but the one true athletic freak I played with was Brandon Rush. I'm usually not good at singling things out, but Brandon was the best athlete I've ever played with. It was almost like boot camp wasn't difficult for him. He could run fast, jump high and never get tired. This is going to sound like I'm exaggerating, but I'm telling you, Brandon Rush did not sweat. We would run and run and run in boot camp, and he might not necessarily win every single sprint, but people are puking in trash cans and collapsing at the finish line and you'd look at Brandon and he would look like ... this is it?

In practices, if you get in trouble for something, they put you on a treadmill and crank the speed and incline up to as high as it will go. It's intense. Some guys go flying off the end of it. Brandon would be on the treadmill at the highest elevation and the highest speed and he could just go and go and go. If you ever watched our huddles during timeouts, you would notice that Brandon never sat down. Now, most guys who play basketball at that level are exceptionally good athletes and are in great shape. But we get tired. You play as hard as you can for a couple minutes, then come over for a timeout exhausted. Not Brandon. He'd just stand there. He was fine. I've never seen anything like it.

Anyway, keeping yourself in great shape was really important for boot camp, and not just for your own benefit. See, when we're running the 20s – you run baseline to baseline twice in 20 seconds, and you have to do this 20 times – if one person doesn't make their time, or misses a line, the sprint doesn't count for the whole team. You have to do it until the entire team has successfully completed 20 of these. I think the most we ever did in my career was 34. So you can imagine what happens when a guy doesn't make his time. The rest of us will do whatever it takes to get him to do it. Sometimes he gets yelled at. "Run harder!" "Why are you missing lines?!" That kind of thing. But sometimes effort isn't the problem. Sometimes a guy just can't do it, which means we're running, say, sprint No. 16 over and over again. In those cases, one of the guys who are in better shape – Brady, Tyshawn, and I were always in pretty good shape – will literally carry him across the line so he can make his time. It really puts you through the ringer as a team.

Guys try to do anything they can to get the slightest advantage. My freshman year, in the middle of the workout, Darrell Arthur took off his clothes. Not all of them, but almost. He stripped off his shirt, and his shorts, so that he was running in compression shorts and shoes and that was it. It was funny, but we were mostly too tired to laugh.

Because I had run track in high school, the running didn't scare me that much and I handled it pretty well. My freshman year, there were some stories written about how I had won most of the sprints and that my teammates were impressed. Certainly part of it was that my track career had physically prepared me for this. But another part was that

I just simply wanted to win the sprints. I was competitive about it. Tyshawn Taylor and I had a lot of battles over the years in the sprints. He's really fast, too, and we were always pushing each other. I would definitely say that Tyshawn is quicker than me laterally and in short bursts, my only chance was in a long full-court sprint. I think it was good for us.

Generally speaking, I think boot camp is tougher on big guys. Some of the stuff we have to do, like the defensive stance, just isn't something big men do on a regular basis. Besides, they're just bigger. I will say, though, that Chase Buford was notorious for vomiting. A lot of guys threw up during this, and there were trash cans all around the court for just that reason, but Chase became known for it. One year, some of the coaches thought it would be funny to plaster his picture on some of the trash cans around the gym. Sure enough, the next morning when we arrived at boot camp the managers were out early taping his face to all of them. The thing is, throwing up doesn't offer you any relief from the drills. You just puke, then start running again.

—◆—

Tyrel shattered his roommate's conception of what was possible regarding human pizza intake.

—◆—

Tyrel, on the other hand, was blessed with a highly active metabolism. Curt Welter, who was his roommate during Tyrel's senior year, has seen him put away a great deal of candy and Dr. Pepper.

But he describes one instance at CiCi's, a buffet pizza chain, in which Tyrel shattered Welter's conception of what was possible regarding human pizza intake.

"I knew he could eat a ton, because of how many calories he burns in a day," Welter said. "He didn't have a game coming up for a while. It was during a break and he wasn't going to have to practice. I talked him into seeing how much pizza he could eat. I did it, too. I think I ate 14 slices. I felt sick leaving there. He ate like 26 slices of pizza and he ate four brownies, too. Thirty pieces of food that day. It was unreal.

"The next day, he went to work out. He might have sweated a little bit more, but it didn't affect his workout. The kid can eat. I was in shock how much food he put down that night. I've never seen anybody even get close to that number."

—◆—

There are two high-anxiety events for freshmen basketball players at Kansas. Boot camp is the first one. Late Night in the Phog is the second one. Nobody tends to puke at Late Night, but when you realize you are going to be performing in front of 16,300 people for the first time, you get that uneasy feeling in your gut. Because it's not just basketball (although there is basketball), it's dancing.

Late Night is on a Friday night, so on Tuesday you begin rehearsing your dance routine. Each class has a different routine. You go in there and work with the dance team and they come up with something. Tuesday is about getting instructed on what to do. Wednesday is about practicing it, then you go in Thursday and if you've got it down, you're good to go. My freshman year, we wanted to keep it pretty simple so we wouldn't screw it up.

Just like with the autographs, just like with boot camp, the upper classmen try to make this as uncomfortable for you as possible. "Hey, better not mess up, man." "You're gonna be nervous." "Don't choke." Thanks, fellas.

My first year we all showed up in Hummers and all these fancy cars, wearing suits. It was a red carpet theme. We got interviewed on the red carpet outside the Fieldhouse, then came inside for our routines.

I don't consider myself much of a dancer, but fortunately for me, I had a 6'11" goofball in my class. Not only were all eyes on him anyway, no matter how bad of a dancer I was, Cole was 10 times worse.

The next day, somewhat mercifully, practice begins.

Because of the way my freshman year ended, a lot of people probably forget that it began with quite a bit of uncertainty.

Granted, we had a really good team coming back. We had talent. We had veterans. We had depth at every spot. We had experience deep in the tournament.

We also had a star player with a ruptured ligament in his knee.

I felt really bad for Brandon. He had declared for the draft after the previous season, and there was no doubt he was good enough to play in the NBA. He was about to live his dream, and then he tore his ACL. Fortunately for him, he hadn't hired an agent, so he was eligible to come back to Kansas. I'm sure this was disappointing to him in a lot of ways, but you would have never known it by watching him. He was so unfazed by anything, and he worked extremely hard to rehabilitate his knee in time for his junior year to start.

This was the big storyline in the media going into that season. Brandon was such an important part of our team, and there is so much interest in Kansas basketball, that his injury really became a big story.

And I will get to all that. But before I do, I will address another of the storylines in the media going into that year, which was the extent to which I was or was not like Kirk Hinrich.

This wasn't something I put a whole lot of thought into, but it was a comparison some people seemed to want to make. I guess I would have to say it was flattering in a way. I mean, Kirk was a four-year starter at Kansas and had been the No. 7 pick in the NBA draft. His jersey is now hanging from the rafters in Allen Fieldhouse. He was a great player. I suppose it is cool that people are interested enough in you to make a comparison, though I suspect that a major reason for this comparison was that Kirk and I are both 6'3" white guards with dark hair who played at Kansas. I was a completely unproven freshman and was nowhere near his level. I'm not sure that was a great comparison.

Though I began the season unproven, I got an opportunity to prove myself early because Brandon was hurt. You would never wish an injury like that on anybody, and I was just as happy as anyone when he got back because I knew how important he was to our team, but it is true that his injury allowed me to get some playing time I probably would not otherwise have gotten.

The most difficult thing for a freshman is to get a grasp of the offense. There is a lot of freedom within Coach Self's offense, which is both what makes it great and what makes it difficult. You have a lot of decisions to make, and you have to understand the timing of it. Timing is so important in Coach Self's offense because everything is on a string. A move by one guy triggers a move by another guy. As I discussed earlier in the book, the timing is a big reason you don't want to be dribbling the way I did as a freshman, back when I was High School Hondo.

I tried hard to learn it, talking to coaches to try to figure it out. I think this was a big reason I got to play while Brandon was out. That first game, I've got all the nerves you would imagine. I don't remember who I checked in for, but when I was running to the scorer's table to check in for the first time, I remember double checking that I had my jersey on underneath my warm-ups. Since the jersey is the last thing we put on before we take the floor, this is a more realistic concern than you might realize. Brandon actually forgot to put his on one time. They were announcing the starting lineups when he realized it, so a manager went running back into the locker room to get it for him. He ended up getting it on before tipoff.

—◆—

Without Rush in the lineup, Kansas started Darrell Arthur, Sasha Kaun, Mario Chalmers, Sherron Collins, and Russell Robinson in the 2007 season opener.

Tyrel was the third guard off the bench behind Rodrick Stewart and Jeremy Case. His first statistical act as a Kansas basketball player was grabbing an offensive rebound, which he converted into a layup with 15 minutes left in the second half. He scored 11points on 4-for-5 shooting while playing 11 minutes.

Collins led KU with 22 points and six assists in a 107-78 Kansas win.

Self, typically, decided to make a point of the 78.

"That's as poor of a defensive performance as we've had in a long time," he said after the game. "To give up 78 in your own building … first one to 70 should always win. I thought our guards didn't guard their guards at all tonight."

But Self was impressed with Reed's performance.

"If Tyrel can go against Rod and Sherron and Russell and Mario every day, then he's gonna be pretty good in the game," Self said.

—◆—

Early that year, I was often the first or second guard off the bench, depending on how Coach Self subbed Rodrick Stewart and me. It felt like I usually came in about the 14-minute mark of the first half.

My goal when I got onto the floor was to basically do the right thing on offense and defense and stay out of the veterans' way. You want to make a play when you can, but you also understand you're on a veteran team that knows what it's doing and it's all running through them. You want to make sure the team doesn't get worse with you out there. That sounds like a really simple and obvious point, but it's the right way to look at it. Coach Self says that all the time. "Why would I ever put you in if the team gets worse with you on the floor?" So that was the goal. Don't be that guy.

Things were going well for me. I was getting to play, and I felt fortunate about that. When I signed with KU, I knew it was going to be a real challenge for me to earn minutes on a team that experienced, which was totally fine with me. I didn't expect to play a ton of minutes as a freshman, in part because Coach Self told me that.

That said, it felt great being out there, playing in front of 16,300, living the dream. I can't say this enough, but Kansas has the best fans in the country, hands down.

Brandon played against Washburn and Northern Arizona, our third and fourth games of the season, but his first big game back was against Arizona in the Fieldhouse. On the last play of the first half, Jerryd Bayless of Arizona had gotten a steal and I was trying to get back to stop the play. I went underneath him and fell down. Meanwhile, Darnell Jackson blocked the shot off the backboard and all 250 pounds of him fell on my ankle. It was hurting pretty badly, but it wasn't like I could just lay there on the floor – it was halftime. So I hobbled as quickly as I could back out the tunnel into the locker room. I knew I was going to be done for a while. They called it a severe sprain. That was November 25. I didn't play in a game again until December 5 against Eastern Washington.

That game more or less marked the end of my time in the regular rotation that year. The timing was pretty crazy that way. Just as Brandon was back to playing full time, I was hurt. Even after I healed, I knew Brandon was going to be playing most of the minutes, which has a domino effect down the lineup. Coach Self also starts to tighten his rotation the closer we get to conference play. I completely understood that this was the way it was going to be and just wanted to continue to get better in practice and help the team any way that I could.

— ◆ —

People probably remember the 2007 team as a deep team, which it was. But if you really look at it, KU wasn't using a deep rotation at all. By the end of the year, it was basically this:

Starters	Bench
G – Russell Robinson	*F – Sasha Kaun*
G – Mario Chalmers	*G – Sherron Collins*
G – Brandon Rush	
F – Darrell Arthur	
F – Darnell Jackson	

Because of his big moments in the Final Four and the player he became the next season, people may remember Aldrich as being a bigger part of the rotation than he was. He averaged only 8.3 minutes per game. Rodrick Stewart played in 33 of the 40 games. Tyrel played in 23 games, averaging 6.3 minutes. Jeremy Case played in 30 games. Outside of the top seven, Aldrich was the only other player who played in every game.

— ◆ —

Our first big road test that year was at Southern Cal, which had O.J. Mayo, who was one of the top players in that class. Even though we players don't follow recruiting much, we definitely know who O.J. Mayo is. Just like how NBA players I'm sure get a little extra juiced to play LeBron James, we get a little extra excited to play somebody like O.J.

It was a real grinder of a game. Tim Floyd was USC's coach at the time, and his teams were known for playing gritty games like that.

That game was a test in a lot of ways. Not only was it our first game of the season away from Lawrence, we got behind for the first time that year and got into a pressurized late-game situation for the first time.

We were up by two points in the final minute, but the clock was such that unless we got an offensive rebound on a miss, USC was going to get another possession. We really needed to score. With a few seconds left on the shot clock, Mario took a deep three-pointer that probably wasn't a very good shot at the time. I'm guessing Coach Self was thinking that was a terrible shot so late in the clock, but once it went in I think all was forgiven. We didn't know it at the time, of course, but there was some foreshadowing in that shot.

We had a couple other tough road games that year. We won a close one at Georgia Tech, and played really well at Boston College, blowing them out.

Our record was 20-0 when we went to Manhattan to play K-State. We had never lost in Bramlage Coliseum before, and it was 24 years old. Now that I think about it, that's pretty crazy. Bramlage was always the toughest arena I played in, and I have no idea how those teams that came before us never lost there.

We went over there expecting to win, just the same as we expect to win every game. But I think K-State had no doubts they were going to win that game. They had Michael Beasley and Bill Walker and it was supposed to be a big year for K-State.

Well, it was their night. The building was so loud and they played really well. Beasley went 4-for-4 from the three-point line. It wasn't like we didn't know he could shoot, but deep shooting was not a big part of his game. Walker made some threes, too. It was like I said with the Memphis game, you always believe you can win, but there are moments when it occurs to you that it just might be the other team's night.

I know a lot of KU fans feel like players make shots against us they wouldn't even take against most teams. If you look for examples of it, you can make that point. But I really don't buy that. I think the same thing when I'm playing FIFA on PS3 with one of my buddies. He'll get a goal and I'm like, "Are you kidding me? You're making that? That's a joke." You feel like this only happens to you. But I'm sure K-Staters feel like we always make shots against them we wouldn't make against other teams, too. That's just the way it feels. I don't think that's reality.

That was January 30. We lost again at Texas on February 11 in a game I don't think there is much to say about. Texas had a really good team and outplayed us in their building that night. There wasn't anything all that remarkable about it, which seems to be unusual with KU-UT games.

The one that really shook us was two games later, at Oklahoma State. We always seem to struggle there, and I can't completely explain that, although I can offer a few insights into this:

- Like most arenas, there are two levels. Unlike most arenas, the upper level at Gallagher-Iba feels like it is right on top of you because of the way they designed it. It kind of hangs over a little bit and it just feels different.
- The fans show up. This cannot be ignored, because it doesn't happen everywhere. I always respected the schools that would fill their arenas.
- The rims are orange, and so is the background. Maybe this is an excuse I shouldn't be using, but as a shooter I always noticed that the shirts everybody wears in the background are almost the exact same color as the rim. I would like to think it throws you off a little bit.

The week leading up to that game was a tough one for us, especially Darnell. He had been through a lot of tragedies already in his life, and his cousin had been killed earlier in the week. Sherron was hurt too, and didn't play much (11 minutes). (Oklahoma State's) Byron Eaton just kept driving on us and getting to the line. We lost by one.

It is tough to say for sure how much Darnell's situation affected us. I can tell you things like that can definitely have an effect on a team's performance. Sports are all about focus, so anything that distracts you from the game can hurt you.

You usually don't know for sure why you didn't play well, but we just didn't. We got behind and made a comeback, but not quite enough of one.

That loss shook us up a little bit. We realized we weren't invincible, and one of the outcomes was the realization some things needed to be said, some things needed to be heard and we needed to sort it all out as a team. The manifestation of this was that some guys on the team – I can't remember who – decided we ought to go to Henry T's for dinner as a team, an event which I am now aware has taken on something of a legendary quality. I assume this is at least partially because nobody outside the team knows exactly what happened there, except that we never lost again that season.

So here's the story: Henry T's is a sports bar known for its wings and burgers. It has one extra large booth in one of the corners, which suited us fine. There was nothing "official" about this meeting. It was just sort of like, "Hey, we're going to Henry T's," and everybody showed up.

I imagine the other people in the restaurant were pretty curious about all this. Because we all have different schedules, it's pretty rare to see the entire basketball team in the same place at the same time unless we're playing in a game or something. But there we all were. The idea was that if you had something to say, this was the time to say it. If you had some issue with a teammate or a coach, get it off your chest here and now. You could say whatever you wanted to say, no holds barred. I don't remember many specifics of the conversation, but, to be honest, the content of the conversation was less important than the mere existence of the conversation. In other words, what we said mattered less than the fact we were saying things.

—◆—

Aldrich said the meeting was the product of urgency.

"(Stuff) hit the fan," he said. "It was like, 'What's going on now?' We should have never had those thoughts, because we were still a very good team that just went through a little slump. Darnell and I just kind of made up the little plan of going to Henry T's. Everybody talked. Everybody shared their own views of what we needed to do. I think it came down to guys stopping making excuses and starting to do what they know to do."

It was not an entirely relaxing dinner.

"I would say it was laid back, but it was confrontational a little bit," Aldrich said. "I think that's why we were so good as a team. We definitely had some voices on the team, with Darnell and Russell and Mario. You have to have that to be able to grow as a team. If Russell's not doing his job, Mario needs to say something to Russell. If Mario's not doing his job, Russell needs to say something to Mario, just to keep everybody in check. That team was so tight. Guys felt they could do those things, they could say, 'Hey, you know what, you didn't play worth a (crap), so next game we need to do a lot better."

—◆—

I think it was a turning point. Everybody understood how everybody was feeling. There might have been a little animosity and guys were maybe saying stuff to other people instead of coming out in front of everybody and saying how they felt.

It wasn't like we were there for three hours discussing our problems. It was a 45-minute meal and we were out. It was a little thing, but sometimes little things like that make a difference, and I think it did. I think we grew closer that night.

I wouldn't expect people to fully understand what that was all about. There are probably 3,000 different stories going around, and although I don't think it happened in this case, sometimes players like to kind of mess with the media a little bit, or say something they don't understand.

That said, I feel like that loss and our reaction to it, including the Henry T's meeting, was a turning point for us. We had lost two out of our last three games, and all three of our losses had come between January 30 and February 23. It was humbling. We felt like we had to get it turned around or the wheels could possibly fall off. Guys changed their mentality, and we didn't lose again.

We beat Iowa State in Ames in our next game, and then it was on to the rematch with K-State. Allen Fieldhouse was on fire that night. So loud. It's like that any time we play K-State, but I think the fans were a little extra pumped because Michael Beasley had said they were going to beat us in Manhattan, they were going to beat us in Lawrence, and they were going to beat us in Africa. Now, as players, we're all the same age and we realize we say dumb things at times. I'm guessing Mike would like to have that one back. Or maybe he wouldn't. I don't know. At any rate, it turned him into an even bigger target for our fans than he already was (which was pretty big).

—◆—

This was just Kansas' night. The Wildcats scored the first two points of the game but never led again. KU got up by 24 in the second half and won 88-74.

Remarkably, Beasley scored 39 points and had 11 rebounds. Brandon Rush led KU with 21. Tyrel didn't play.

—◆—

That just shows you how good Beasley was. He came into the Fieldhouse as a freshman and scored 39. I missed Kevin Durant, but my teammates would talk about how tough he was to deal with. Beasley was like that. He was just so smooth. I'm always amazed when freshmen can play at that level, because it is really difficult. It is a difficult transition for almost all of us. Whenever I see a guy dominate like that as a freshman, it blows me away.

It always does feel a little bit better to beat K-State and Missouri for all the obvious reasons. But I'm pretty sure I feel a little bit differently about it than the average fan does. For one thing, I know most of the players on K-State's roster personally. I worked camps with Jacob Pullen and Denis Clemente. Those guys are my friends. So there isn't any bad blood. I actually root for K-State when they are playing anyone except us, and I was even like that growing up. I was a KU fan, but I wanted K-State to do well. They're an in-state team and I love the state of Kansas. I suppose there might be more people out there like me than is commonly realized. With Missouri, it is a little different. It goes back to the Civil War and it's always there. It's not a good relationship.

Two days later, we played Texas Tech, and it was senior night and, well, we had it going that night.

We had one more chance for a revenge game that year, and it came in the Big 12 championship game against Texas. I don't know what it is, but something about that UT-KU rivalry makes for great games. That both teams always have great players is a big part of it, I guess, but still, it always seems like something memorable happens.

The memorable thing about that game was how well both teams played. It was almost surreal to watch. You're sitting on the bench and you never know when you're going to be called on, but you're sitting there watching it, just amazed. It was great basketball being played. I don't know how many NBA players were on the court at that time, but it was a lot. We were playing great defense, they were hitting big shots. Same way for us. If you're a basketball fan, that had to be fun to watch because of the pure skill and talent on display. That's one of the better halves of basketball that I've witnessed.

The NCAA Tournament is a totally different animal from the regular season. You get funky game times, you don't know who you're going to play. It's weird. The stands are often half full and even the half that is there is a mix of a few different teams' fans. You have to bring your own energy to the game. Playing in Allen Fieldhouse, we're spoiled. Once the game tips off, it's not that hard to get going. You talk to other players around the country and they love coming to the Fieldhouse and playing. They may only play in front of a half-full house at home. Everything about the tournament has a different feel.

We played Portland State in the first round of my freshman year. You know they're everybody's underdog and you've got to fight that the whole time. Everybody wants them to win. It may mess up their bracket, but it's fun when the underdog wins. That's just how it is.

Nonetheless, we played pretty well against Portland State. Then we had a nice game against UNLV and whipped Villanova pretty hard in the Sweet 16. Which put us in the Elite Eight, where we had lost the year before, against Davidson, who was everybody's Cinderella story.

As much as you try to ignore everything, there are certain facts that people just won't let you forget. We were aware that all of Coach Self's best tournament runs had ended in the Elite Eight. It had happened to him at Tulsa, Illinois, and twice at Kansas. And we were also dealing with the Cinderella thing. Everybody wanted them to win, and they were on a roll. They may have had some regrettable losses during their conference year, but by that point they could have beaten anyone. Stephen Curry was great, and they had another guard that was very good and a big guy, also.

What you try to do is get in the mindset that you can't wish anything to happen. You can't wish yourself into the Final Four. You have to go take it. Coach Self says that a lot. But you hear something a hundred times from reporters or fans, whether you say you're going to think about it or not, it's still there. You may not think about it at the time, but it may cause some doubt somewhere in your mind.

There is a lot of pressure to perform well. Not just at Kansas, either. But you really feel those NCAA Tournament losses. You feel like you're letting people down. You may not want to show your face in

Lawrence for a while, but you've got to be a man and step out there, go get food, go to the grocery store regardless and know that's not going to define you as a person. I mean, they can bet on us out in Vegas. There are things going on outside of our world. It's crazy to think we can't get paid but other people can make money off of us.

Anyway, we played like we felt the pressure that night. It was a tight, low-possession game. Neither team really performed like it had been. Curry didn't have a good shooting night (9-for-25), but you had to respect his shot no matter where he was on the floor. He had such deep range, so you had to be up in him and everybody else had to be in strong help behind you. I felt like we had guys who could guard anybody in the country. With Mario, Russell, and Brandon, we could deal with any perimeter player we needed to.

On the last possession, we put Brandon on Curry. He was our best overall defender and we were pretty sure Curry was going to be taking the shot. But Brandon fell down, Mario took Curry and he passed it off to their other guard, who put up a long three that would have won it. I was on the sideline, which, by the way, was a really weird sideline. The floor was elevated to the point that the court was at about chest level. Coach Self sat on a stool up on the floor. It was just crazy. Those games were at Ford Field in Detroit, which is this gigantic football field they plopped a basketball floor onto. It didn't feel intimate at all. Anyway, I'm sitting there, leaning out, and it looked like that shot was going in. My heart was thumping. I think Coach Self's was, too. He collapsed to the floor. I can only imagine what a weight was lifted off his shoulders.

The locker room was funny. When we got in there, we were all calm and cool. Coach Self walked in there and he was like, "What are you guys doing? Let's celebrate." He was jumping around, we threw a bucket of water on him, we started throwing water on each other. It probably got out of hand and we had to stop. We always take it a little too far.

I guess Darnell said Coach Self teared up. I don't remember him bawling or anything, but there were definitely those emotions overtaking him at that time. I can only imagine coaching in college basketball for so long and coming so close. You're so defined by that last game in college. I think we need to be held accountable for losing in the NCAA Tournament, but we try not to let it define us as a team. Things happen. It's tough when people say we had a bad season. You wish it wouldn't be that way, that you went 35-3 but didn't have a good year. I think at a lot of places that would be a pretty good year.

The Davidson win was really a pressure release in a lot of ways. I felt like once we got to the Final Four, there was a sense of calmness.

"Have I not commanded you? Be strong and courageous. Do not be afraid; do not be discouraged, for the LORD your God will be with you wherever you go."

Joshua 1:9

Sophomore Year

Technically, the period between October 15, 2007, and October 15, 2008, was not longer than any other year. But that did not stop it from seeming like the longest year ever.

Think about it. I got in as a freshman not knowing much, which made for a long summer because I had never been through it before. Then, by winning the national title, we had the longest season possible. And then we went to Canada in August of my sophomore year. Then we had a whole new season. My freshman and sophomore years feel like one big year in a way. It's hard to say when one ended and the other began.

Whatever people wanted to call it – rebuilding year, young team, down year – it described us in 2008-09. This is not to say we didn't think we were going to be good. We always think that, and we always expect to win every game and we expect to win the Big 12 title. Those expectations never change.

But we had lost almost all of our key players from the national title team. The only returning player who averaged more than 10 minutes per game was Sherron. From a fan's perspective, everyone thought the cupboard was bare.

———◆———

"Going into my sophomore year, a lot of people were saying we were going to be Florida when Florida won the back-to-back championships and didn't even make the tournament the next year, with Carolina doing the same thing after we won it," Aldrich said. "We heard all those things about Florida and we were like that's not going to be us. We're a much better team than that."

———◆———

As players, the mindset was that now it was our turn to step up and play. Coach Self always talks about the cycle. Players come, players go. Some years there are going to be a lot more leave than another. We were all confident in ourselves, but you don't know how we're all going to react when we get out there as a team. You've seen each other in practice and in pickup games, but until you actually step on the floor in a real game, you never really know how good you are or what kind of a team it's going to be.

I thought that was a good year to take that trip to Canada. Because we were inexperienced, we needed as many live game situations as possible. I think it helped us once the season started, because we had already established a lot of the groundwork with our offense and our defense, some of our plays, how the coaches coach.

The Canada trip was great in that sense, but it wasn't so great in that it occurred in August, and we had 10 days of practice before we left. By the way, Allen Fieldhouse doesn't have air conditioning.

It was brutal. Long hours in August when you're usually back home getting that break between summer classes and fall classes, and you didn't get that. At first it was tough. Some guys didn't want to be there. Once you got going, you realized this was a time we could get better. It did help us out. We about lost to one team in the Alaska tournament, and had to fight through some adversity. That just showed how much uncertainty there was for us that year. After we almost lost that game, Coach Self was like, "I didn't know what was going to happen."

One of the other challenges for us on that trip was playing without Sherron. He had knee surgery that offseason and had come back from break a little heavier than Coach Self wanted. So the plan was not to play him in Canada unless he really thought Sherron could help us. I think he wanted to see what we would be like without Sherron ... but Sherron obviously helped out.

At that point, Sherron had not yet established himself as the leader everybody remembers. He had been at KU for two years, but had come off the bench most of that time. Even though everybody knew he was a really good player, being a really good player doesn't necessarily make you a leader. Now, Sherron was a leader, as it turned out. He was really good at it. But you have to see it first. You don't just lead with your play, but with how you treat people off the court, how you are with your teammates. Sherron was good. He was a guy people looked up to, and he could take pressure. If we'd lose, everybody would turn to him. He embraced that.

Sherron could lighten a room or darken a room by how he was feeling when he walked in. He was definitely moody, and that's not necessarily a bad thing. Sometimes you've got to be in a bad mood for others to mean business. But he was so balanced and kept us all calm.

Stubbornness is one of the things that makes Sherron who he is. He has an opinion on everything and he's not just going to agree with you to agree. Coach Self liked that. He also carried himself well. He carried himself confidently, but not cocky. He hated to lose. He was a fierce competitor. He is a lot like Coach Self, actually, and I think that helped. Things go a lot more smoothly when the point guard and the coach are on the same wavelength.

He took on a lot of pressure and responsibility that year. We were so unproven. To start the year, we were scared. We knew we could step on the floor and get blown out if we didn't play well. We went up to Michigan State and got embarrassed, to say the least. By the time that season was over, we felt that we had Michigan State beat and sort of gave them the game.

We really didn't get over that fear of getting blown out until conference play started. The Michigan State game was our last game before Big 12 play, but we had also lost to Arizona, Syracuse, and UMass that season. The UMass loss became kind of a big thing. It was probably because it was our only loss to a team from a smaller conference, but also because of some haircuts. Sherron and Tyshawn had come out for that game with some art in their hair. Sherron had a star shaved into his. They both had little Mohawk looks. We lost, and the haircuts were gone pretty soon. Here was the deal on that: Coach Self is a bit superstitious. If that's how you wear your hair, then wear your hair like that all the time. If you have facial hair, keep your facial hair like that. You don't want it to be something people are talking about. Coach wants everyone to look the same. You'll notice nobody ever did any crazy facial hair, nobody ever does any weird hair. You kind of stay the same the whole season. If you wear a calf sleeve or an arm sleeve, you have to wear it in practice every day. So Travis Releford always wears his two wrist bands every day in practice.

But that wasn't why we lost the game by any means. I felt that it became a bigger deal to everyone outside of the team than it really was.

The Michigan State loss was kind of like the Oklahoma State loss from the year before in that it revealed some things to us. It was a toughness thing. We were trying to make up the character of our team. We knew being prima donnas wasn't going to work. Trying to beat people on talent alone wasn't going to work. If we were going to be better, it was going to be because we were tougher, we were going to guard. It was a terrible loss, but it was good that it was our last non-conference game. We knew that chapter was over; we can put that aside.

Coach definitely looks at the season as a build-up to conference play, and then a build-up to March.

One of the biggest reasons for our success that year was Cole's development. When he started out as a freshman, you definitely could have said he wasn't as good as the other big guys on our team.

He just wasn't as polished, and didn't understand the game quite yet. He improved so much during his freshman year, then worked really hard during that next summer. I think because he is so carefree and enjoys life so much, it was easy for him to step into a new and bigger role. He just didn't feel the pressure. He never thought of it like that. He just enjoyed it for what it was.

Cole had a triple double against Dayton. He had 13 points, 20 rebounds, and 10 blocked shots, which was the first official triple double in KU history.

He and Sherron were the two go-to guys, so they got lumped together a lot. No matter what was happening, people turned to them. They had a good relationship. It was like anyone else's on the team. There was nothing unusual about it. They had their arguments, just like we had our arguments with them. They were honest and open about things and talked about whatever needed to be talked about.

Cole's game had come the furthest on offense. Defensively, he had a knack for the ball. He had good timing as a shot blocker and a great feel for rebounding. But offensively, he was a bit raw as a freshman. Working with Coach Manning helped a lot, because Coach Manning was never the highest flyer or anything. He is so skilled and knows so much about the game, it helps our big guys to be coached by him. Cole was knocking down jump shots his sophomore year and playing like the star we all knew he was.

Another key for us was the Morris twins. They came in with a class that included Tyshawn, Mario Little, Travis Releford, Quintrell Thomas, and Tyrone Appleton. I don't think it's unfair to say they were a bit lazy as freshmen. They came in not yet knowing how to work hard, not understanding what it took to be a college basketball player. We didn't think they were going to make it through boot camp. Once they did, they just kept progressing on everything. They kept working harder and understanding what it was going to take. I hate lumping them together, but they made the greatest strides of anybody I played with at KU if you look at where they started and you see the finished product. They really worked at it. They worked with Coach Manning and really used college as a stepping stone to get better. That's how college should be.

You could see they had the physical gifts to play in the NBA and they honed their skills to becoming NBA players.

But that freshman year, they didn't even dunk all that much. They definitely could, but it was a mindset thing. Coach wants our big guys to dunk everything around the rim, and I think they had been more like finesse outside players in high school. It took a little bit of time being around our coaches for them to realize that's not going to fly around here. They took it really hard from Coach. I think that helped them develop thicker skin to realize he was going to be that way with them and they had to learn how to take it. One of the things I learned to live by was to listen to what the coaches say, not how they say it.

The twins were tough guys. They're from a tough place. They're competitive. They were never going to let people push them around. Toughness was never an issue with them, but there's a different kind of toughness they had to develop. That toughness might be bringing it every day in practice or finishing around the basket, not getting pushed under the basket for a rebound. Things you don't think are toughness things, but really are. They just didn't understand that yet.

That was the only thing they really lacked at that point.

Now, Markieff is extremely explosive. Just standing there, he can jump about as high as anybody. He's strong, too. Marcus is more of an open-court dunker. Both of them are extremely smart, funny dudes. They want to say things that get people talking and thinking and laughing. I really enjoyed them. They're some of my favorite teammates I'll talk to for the rest of my life. The twins are even smarter on the court. The twins' and Sherron's basketball IQs are off the charts. Great passers, understood where to be, how to make things flow.

Tyshawn was another big part of it, because we needed a ball-handling guard. He, of course, ended up starting most of that year in part because he's extremely athletic, but also because I think he did a good job of understanding what we needed from him and what he could contribute. When you're young and you're not as refined offensively, you've got to be great defensively. I think he did a really good job of using his length and his speed. He adds a different element, an extra option for the way we can approach teams. He speeds up everything. I think that's what Coach Self really likes about him and makes him such a great player. He's so fast, he's slithery, can fit through little spaces, has long arms. He did a remarkable job of being our motor that season.

So all of that was there. We had some nice pieces. But it was a process putting it together. By the time conference play began, we were pretty close. We opened Big 12 play at home against K-State, and played great. We got up 18-0 and won comfortably. Beating a rival made for a nice start. We got to 8-0 in league play, lost at Missouri, then won four more in a row, including a win at Kansas State, a win over Missouri, and a big win over Oklahoma. OU was No. 3 in the country at the time and we were tied with them for the Big 12 lead at 11-1.

Blake Griffin was out that night with a concussion, which actually disappointed all of us. We wanted him to play. You always want to beat somebody when they're at their best. It kind of makes me mad, but I never really got to face Blake. He hurt himself pretty early in the game at the Fieldhouse the year before, and left for the NBA after his sophomore year. He was such a great player in college, and now in the pros, and I missed out on playing him for those two years.

Sherron went off that game. He was knocking down 30-footers. Tyshawn had his career high (26) that game. It was a tough game, even with Blake out.

The reason you want to face a team when they're at their best is pretty simple: You don't want there to be any doubts about it. It gives you that much more satisfaction when you beat somebody at their best. People may still have doubts about us in that game. Would we have beaten them? Well, he wasn't able to play, so there's not much you can talk about. I'd like to think that we would still have won that game.

It wasn't that the Oklahoma game gave us the Big 12 title, but it is true that we were 12-1 after that, meaning we were in really good

In order to fly for road games we take a bus from Lawrence to Forbes Field in Topeka.

shape with a home game against Missouri, a road game against Texas Tech, and a Senior Night game against Texas in Lawrence left on the schedule. We blew out Missouri, lost to Texas Tech by 19 on their Senior Night, and beat Texas by 10. We were Big 12 champs again and feeling good heading into the conference tournament.

I don't know what it is, but we always had a tendency to not play well in the first round of the Big 12 tournament. The year before, we had struggled with Nebraska in the first round, and it was the same story this time against Baylor. I'm not saying Baylor wasn't a good team, because they always have talented guys, but I am saying we didn't play like we were capable of playing.

It was a real letdown when we lost to Baylor. We break the season up into nonconference, conference, conference tournament, and NCAA tournament. It was the longest bus trip back, too. The tournament was in Oklahoma City that year, and the weather was terrible and snowy. The roads were slick. We drove about 30 miles per hour the whole way home on this big bus. It took all night. The whole thing was unpleasant. We had just lost in the first round, we were feeling like we shouldn't have lost, and it gave us extra practice time leading up to the NCAA Tournament. Those were grueling practices, mentally and physically. During that time of year it's nice to have shorter practices, but it definitely helped us out in the long run.

One thing people should understand is that we really did think we could win the national championship. Even though the season began with so much uncertainty, even though we had gotten embarrassed at Michigan State, even though we were young, we feel like if you're good enough to win the Big 12 championship, you're good enough to win the national championship. That's the goal every year, regardless of the team we have. Maybe some people outside the program felt like winning the Big 12 title and winning a couple of games in the NCAA Tournament was good enough or even an overachievement, but that's not the way it feels to us.

We didn't impress ourselves by winning the Big 12. It's just something we were proud of. There were so many doubters that year. That was our fifth regular season championship in a row. This is what is done at Kansas and we're going to hold up that standard. I don't know if other teams put as much emphasis on it, but that's a big part of Coach Self's philosophy. If you win your conference, that means you have a chance to win the national championship. You're going to be in the race. That's why we put so much into it. Before we break every huddle we yell, "Big 12 Champs!"

So if you were wondering if we derived any satisfaction from making it to the Sweet 16 and playing a much better game against Michigan State and showing so much improvement from when we had played them in January, the answer is no. I think the loss hurt worse because of that. I mean, we were up five in the last few minutes. We kind of just gave it away. We felt we were the better team at that point. We had gotten better each step of the way and that was going to be another way of showing it, but we gave it away.

— ◆ —

Kansas had a five-point lead with 3:22 left. Michigan State tied the game on a Raymar Morgan dunk with 1:21 left. After a turnover by Sherron Collins, the Spartans got a three-point play when Collins fouled Kalin Lucas on a jump shot, giving MSU a 63-60 lead with 49 seconds left.

The decisive exchange came after Taylor made two free throws to pull KU to within one with 32 seconds left. KU fouled Lucas, who made both shots for a three-point lead. But with 19 seconds left, Michigan State's Travis Walton fouled Collins, sending him to the line for a one-and-one. He missed the front end, Walton got the rebound, and Tyrel fouled Lucas, who made two more free throws to ice it.

It was the only time Tyrel fouled out in his career.

— ◆ —

That felt the same as any other loss to me. I didn't feel any satisfaction because we had improved. It hurt worse because we felt we were the better team and we couldn't quite get it done. In the Elite Eight we would have played Louisville, one of those athletic teams that loves to get up and down. Teams usually try to slow it down on us, so that would have been fun. It would have been a good matchup for us.

Dear Tyrel Reed

I know when you play you can win! I have total confidence that you will win. Without you they having to risk a lot. Go Tyrel you can do it! You can do anything if you put your mind to it.

Consider it pure joy,
my brothers and sisters,
whenever you face trials
of many kinds.

James 1:2

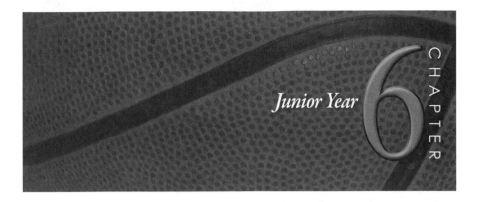

Junior Year 6 CHAPTER

Yeah, I remember the recruitment of the Henry brothers. Like I said before, it's not something we intensely follow, but I knew Xavier had been committed to Memphis and re-opened his recruiting when (Coach) John Calipari left for Kentucky. Coach Self had told us Xavier and C.J. might be joining our team.

We wanted that to happen, because Coach Self wanted it to happen, but we weren't wrapped up in it. As players, we want whatever is going to give us the best chance to win and we knew by getting X, another great player, and C.J. coming with him, it was going to help out. Obviously, I was going to be competing for minutes with him and you have to welcome that. You're at a program where great players come and go. There's always going to be somebody wanting your spot. You have to embrace that and work your tail off. I was never like, "Oh man, he's going to come in and take my minutes." No, you have to prove what you can do on the floor.

It never gets old being No. 1.

Maybe we would have been No. 1 anyway. I don't know. But certainly with X we were No. 1. It's really fun being on the cover of all the magazines. You don't want to think about it, because you don't want to feel like you're protecting something like that, but it never gets old being No. 1. You just wish people wouldn't talk about it as much.

Another thing that I wished people wouldn't have talked about as much were the football-basketball altercations that fall. In a parking lot one day, I think a few guys got into an argument. I don't think it was that big of a deal, but once somebody punches somebody else, you're going to protect your teams. That's just what happens. I wasn't there. I was already in my room because I had already left the training table. It really became a big deal. I guess when you're involved you don't think it's as big of a deal as people outside looking in.

I know in hindsight, it's something you don't want to be involved in as a team and as a university. It put a black eye on the university and became something we had to fight the rest of the year, with people talking about us being a bunch of thugs. I love the University of Kansas with all my heart and know all of my teammates felt the same way. I know we all wish that we could go back and fix that particular incident.

On some level, it was just college kids being college kids. It's a bunch of competitive guys. If it would have been a bunch of kids that got into it at a bar on any college campus, it wouldn't have been a big deal. But it was football vs. basketball at the University of Kansas. It shouldn't have been seen as football vs. basketball. I had great friends on the football team and the whole time it was going on, we were like, "Man, what is going on?" Then you'd say, "I don't know. Why is this such a big deal?"

I still don't know the full story. Some guys obviously had a disagreement and, in the heat of a couple of moments, tried to settle it in a way that caused quite a commotion. It's something I think we all rather would have not dealt with.

That said, it was blown out of proportion in my mind. It was a big deal in that it made the football and basketball teams look bad and made the university look bad. You think about all of our loyal fans and the people giving money to the school, and it hurt them. It hurt recruiting. You don't want that to happen. But from the inside, it wasn't like we felt like we were a part of some big conflict. I mean, my sister ultimately married a football player (Darrell Stuckey) and I'm great friends with the punter, Alonso Rojas.

After that happened, our athletic director at the time, Lew Perkins, came and gave the football and basketball teams a talk. He basically said to put aside whatever petty disagreements we had and look at the big picture. Whenever something bad happens, Coach Self will give us a curfew for a while, but there were never any ultimatums or consequences to come out of it.

Fortunately, basketball season started soon.

The best overall game we played that year was at Temple, which was a really good team. They were a Top 25 team. It was one of those games we were clicking on all cylinders. One of the funny things about that trip was that it was a homecoming for the Morris twins, who lived pretty close to Temple's campus in Philadelphia. Well, I had never been to Philly and had never had a genuine Philly cheesesteak. There was a place in Philadelphia where the twins were going to get our cheesesteaks. It was a big deal, and we didn't get them. Something happened. I think we paid for them and they couldn't get them delivered to us.

They had talked this place up like it was going to be awesome and we didn't even get them. We gave the twins a lot of crap for that.

—◆—

A Sidebar from My Co-Author

It may be a good thing these cheesesteaks were not delivered. Here's why:

I knew there were two rival cheesesteak places in Philly, but I couldn't remember their names. So before that trip, I asked both Marcus and Markieff for the names of these places. "There's Geno's and there's Max's," Marcus told me. "If you're a tourist, you'd probably go to Geno's, but I'd say Max's. Max's is in my neighborhood."

So I land in Philly, get my work done (for the Topeka Capital-Journal*) and decide I'm going to Max's. Well, Max's is in North Philly. The Fresh Prince was from West Philly, which is a bad neighborhood.*

North Philly is one of the worst neighborhoods in the United States. Anyway, it's after dark and I'm driving into North Philly, and I have a decision to make: Am I going to be the scared white guy from Kansas and turn around or am I going to forge on into North Philadelphia and order a sandwich like a man?

So I kept going. I can't say anything about the area felt unsafe, necessarily. This obviously was not a nice neighborhood but I didn't, you know, see any crimes being committed (except some loitering and jaywalking).

I got my cheesesteak without incident and ate it at my hotel. It was pretty good. They used provolone instead of whiz and put ketchup on it, which I thought was weird. You also could order beers to go at Max's, which you don't see in Kansas. I had a fine sandwich, and then spent the next 14 hours between the bed and the bathroom, as my digestive system decided it was time to evacuate. It was food poisoning, and it was awful.

Tipoff was in the early afternoon. I finally got to a place where I could trust my own body about 90 minutes before tip. I haven't had a cheesesteak since.

Turns out the rival cheesesteak places are Geno's and Pat's. Both are in South Philly.

I kept wanting to give the twins a hard time about that, but kept forgetting to. I submitted to Tyrel my theory that they thought it would be funny to send a guy like me into North Philly.

"They wanted you to go into their neighborhood," Tyrel said. "They get satisfaction from doing things like that." – Tully Corcoran

—◆—

We were No. 1 for basically the entire nonconference season, until we lost at Tennessee. Not much about the game itself stands out to me, but I do remember it being a great atmosphere there.

I don't want to say we get tired of being No. 1. You never get tired of being No. 1. It's awesome getting all the added publicity. People talk about you. But it is something you have to deal with. You get tired of people talking about it so much. How does it feel to be No. 1? Do you feel like you're defending something? What's it like being on top? That gets tiring.

—◆—

"Nobody would have thought we'd have the year we did our sophomore year," Aldrich said. "Junior year we had those expectations, so it's a whole different feel around school, around the team. Once people don't expect anything and people do something well, people have high praise."

—◆—

Once you lose, there is no relief in not being No. 1 anymore. It's like, man, we gotta get back to No. 1 again. That's the ultimate quest. You always want to be the best. It's like, "Man, Duke's not better than we are. Why are they No. 2 and we're No. 3?" It's not like we put much into the polls, but you do think those things.

Even though we were ranked high the whole season, outsiders had their doubts. It seemed like one of our most doubted players was Brady Morningstar. I can't say I know exactly why, because he played really well all season, but it seemed like there was something about being a white kid from Kansas that made people question how good he was.

That's just an example of people thinking about our team differently from the way we think about it. To us, it has nothing to do with Brady being from Kansas. Coach Self plays the best players he thinks are going to give us the best opportunity to win, regardless of anything else. Brady got it tough that year from some of the fans. He was producing, putting up good numbers, playing well on the defensive end, doing the things it took for us to win. Some people were probably being too hard on him. He always has a good attitude about it. He's a funny dude who's always cracking jokes. He keeps things light and fresh.

For a couple of kids from Kansas, like Brady and me, it's a dream come true to wear that jersey.

The same thing happened my senior year, when Brady and I started most of the games. Some people didn't think that was going to work. It didn't really irritate me. You understand other people are going to have their own opinions about things. You know what you're capable of as a player. Brady and I didn't look at it as being two white Kansans. We felt like we could have played anywhere and contributed. We had worked hard and were fortunate enough to be put in that situation and help out our senior year. It was a dream come true for him and me. I know our teammates didn't look at it like, "Man, we can't win with these guys." So it's different from the outside looking in.

Most of the attention that year was directed at Sherron, and he was well deserving of it. He was the pulse of our group. Not only was he a great basketball player, he took on so much. It was such a big task. You can understand the media's perception of him with some of the things that happened off the court. But he's genuinely a great person. I think that's why the fans loved him.

One of his little trademarks was that he called everybody his "young fellas." Most of the time, he was referring to younger players like the twins or Tyshawn, but he calls older people that, too. I guess it was his way of commanding respect.

The thing was, even though he was such a big deal, and even though he did command so much respect, and even though he could raise or drop the mood in any room when he walked in, he never big-timed anybody. He was a great teammate. He was always interested in what was going on in your life. He would always ask you what's going on, what you're doing outside of basketball, which is really an important thing when somebody can separate those things and care about you as a person, not just you as a basketball player. If you saw him out in public, you were the biggest thing. He always made you feel that way. There was just something about him. He made others want to follow him and do the things he does. I don't know what the perfect ingredients are for that, but he had them.

Sherron Collins is genuinely a great person.

He was a winner. He was willing to do whatever it took to win. His sophomore year you could have made a case he was the best player on our team at times. He didn't always play the most and he was willing to do those things for the betterment of the team. Finally, his junior and senior years he was ready to take over that role. He was willing to take all the criticism for all us guys and take the hit when things didn't go well. That's what you look for in a leader.

It's important to have somebody who can do that. Players handle criticism from their coaches, from fans, from the media, all in different ways. Some guys can take it better than others. Sherron was able to take that and use it for motivation. He wasn't going to get mad at the media or get mad at Coach for too long. He might be mad for a while, which is understandable, but he got over it and used it as fuel.

—◆—

The team's other primary leader, Aldrich, could see the weight of that season taking its toll on Collins.

"I definitely think he could have handled it better," Aldrich said. "He was the leader of our team and he was the person everybody looked up to for guidance on the court and even in the locker room, but I think he almost put too much pressure on himself. I think he might have had a better season if he would have distributed that and come to me and said, 'Hey, you know what? You gotta help me out.' I would have been way more willing to help him out and take some of that blame because we were looked upon as the leaders. Mainly him, but at the same time I was, and I was kind of the behind-the-scenes, lead-by-action (leader). You never quite know how to go through those things until you do."

By the end of the season, Aldrich felt Collins was fatigued.

"I would say he was tired of dealing with all of it," he said. "He kind of took it personally and said, 'I'm the one that's taking all the blame, even if it's not my fault, it's getting put on me. I could have played a great game and we could have lost and it's still my fault.' That's the territory you take with Coach Self because he trusts his point guard so much and he puts a lot of effort into them to be that leader on the floor."

—◆—

That was something I had to learn to do over time. I had been coached by my dad in high school, and I could always take it from him because he's my dad. But it was different when it was coming from Coach Self. I didn't know how to take it. I took it really hard and really personally. As I got older, Coach Self stressed not to take things personally. I got better at making it water off my back. Earlier, I'd beat myself up. Coach would criticize me and I'd have a bad practice just because of that. By the time I was a senior, I could listen to it, shake my head yeah and move on.

As hard as Tyrel took the criticism, Lacie took it even harder. A team manager, she was at every practice and heard it all. "I took it personally when Tyrel would get yelled at as a freshman," she said. "I was like, 'Oh my gosh, Tyrel is getting yelled at. He's trying really hard!' I was trying to protect him, and at that point it was hard for me to protect him."

Though she was always Tyrel's antagonist as a kid, Lacie grew to see herself as her little brother's protector, and Lacie isn't known for biting her tongue. It is a trait she received from her father and Tyrel did not.

"Lacie has that fire in her," Stacy said. "If somebody says something to her, she's willing to say something back and correct them and give her opinion. Ty is not like that. I wanted my daughter to be that way. I told Darrell (Stuckey), her husband, to be ready. She'll tell you exactly what she thinks when she thinks it. She'll be as honest as the day is long. She'll never lie to you.

"I think they got that competitive fire from me and she got the other side of it. Tyrel just won't say anything bad. He won't confront somebody. He's learning. But if his car has the engine light on he doesn't even like to go to the mechanic about it because he feels like he's confronting them on it."

That being the case, Lacie struggled as she watched her brother absorb the yelling.

"It was hard for me to sit through practice and let him take it," she said. "Especially his freshman year. I got used to it, but it was something that took some time."

Tyrel notes that her saying something wasn't much of an option.

Early in my career, I was afraid of Coach Self.

Lacie has that personality. She's willing to step up and say stuff. I'll take it in, think about it, not say much about it. I don't think she ever would have said anything. She might not have been the manager after that if she did. Coach Self was always very demanding, wanting things done his way, the right way. You respected him for being like that.

That's the part of Coach Self most people don't see. Most people know him as the guy in the press conferences or at the booster club meetings, being funny, being a people person. And he is that guy. He's very good at making the person he's talking to feel like they're the most important person in the room at the time. He's so good at interacting with people. He just has a good balance. Everyone sees the guy who's funny in the press conferences and lighting up the room, and he does that all the time, but when practice time comes around he is one of the most intense, demanding people. He's willing to get on you regardless of who you are, regardless of how good of a player you are. He's going to tell you what he thinks, like it or not. You're gonna listen. He demands that respect from you.

When I was a freshman, I was pretty scared of the guy. I didn't know how to handle him. I thought he was always on me. I wasn't getting much praise, which is understandable. I was a freshman, so I probably wasn't doing much right. I didn't understand where he was coming from. I wished he would treat me more like an upperclassman and give me more leeway. But that's the great thing about him. He knows how to bring you up from freshman year all the way through your senior year. That's why he gets the most out of his players.

— ◆ —

Self, of course, noticed this.

"I think it would have been anybody," Self said. "He was just nervous. He's a pleaser. He didn't want to screw up, and that always drove me nuts about how he didn't want to screw up, and he had to play perfect or be perfect. I think when he finally realized around me all he had to do was just be himself and try real hard. He didn't have to play great, he didn't have to be perfect, he didn't have to make every shot. But what I expected him to do was play with a swagger.

"Toughness is not only physical, it's also mental to the point where you're not looking at the bench. He had to get through that. The first year, people talk about Sherron grew or how other players we've had grew over time. Hey, Tyrel grew a ton. He went from being a guy that was a nervous about screwing up and felt like he couldn't be himself to one of our biggest pranksters and a guy who really loved giving us a hard time. I don't think he could have done that early on."

It wasn't until my junior year that I started to figure him out. I sort of learned it by watching how other guys did it. Brady was always really good at that. He could take something, then dish something back in a fun way that was still respectful.

I think I matured more my senior year than any other year. You become more independent and more aware you're growing up now. You start to understand things a little bit more. I was never like, "Why is he yelling at me?" He wants the best for you. That's going to happen in the workplace. If I continue playing basketball, that's going to happen. You have to be able to take it and not take it personally.

Most of the time, if something happens in practice, you might get yelled at and then it's over. You're not really in trouble. You know you're in trouble when he calls you into his office. Sometimes you can get called in for something good, but if you know you've done something wrong and he calls you into his office, that's probably not a good sign. But he's one of the best people at dealing with situations. He's dealt with so many different things. He has a good way of balancing everything. He has a real knack for making things seem like they aren't as bad as they could be.

He is very balanced as a coach, but I think the thing that really makes him successful is that he is never satisfied. He's never satisfied with what the team does that year. The whole coaching staff is like that. The night we won the national championship, Coach (Joe) Dooley was already talking about next year by the time we got back to the hotel. "Man," he said, "we've got to figure out a way to do that again." KU has won the Big 12 championship seven times in a row, and Coach Self isn't satisfied. He wants eight, nine, and 10.

I'll tell you a story that will hopefully explain him and me a little bit. My freshman year, I was a little fiery at times. The women's team was using the Fieldhouse and the volleyball team was practicing in the volleyball gym, so we couldn't use the Fieldhouse. He said, "I don't know why I'm doing this, but I want to go to the rec and practice." So we go and practice at the rec, where students work out. They could have stood there and watched if they wanted to, but none of them really did. I think they respected us being there. Anyway, we were having a terrible practice. We did shell drill for an hour. On the schedule, it's usually like 10 minutes. And we did it for an hour. He was like, "We can't guard anyone, so if we're not going to get better at least this is going to make me feel better that we're doing this." So we're out there forever. Well, something went wrong. I think a few guys were gone taking a test so they were going to show up late. We didn't have very many guys. Guys were getting tired and people would want a break and it seemed like I was always out there and I was getting frustrated. Coach was yelling at me.

Eventually, I snapped.

I was trying to box out my guy and he got around me and got the ball. Coach Self started yelling at me. The ball was bouncing. I looked at the ball and I knew I was going to punch it, I just didn't know where it was going to go. I punched the ball and it went backward. It zoomed about an inch from Coach's head, and this thing was moving fast. He goes, "I don't know what I would have done to you if that ball would have hit me in the face. But since you didn't hit me in the face, just get on the line and run until I'm tired of watching you."

For the rest of practice, I just ran on the sideline. I probably ran for 30 minutes back and forth. I wasn't sprinting, but I was running at a pace to where he wasn't going to say I wasn't trying. I talked to him about it later, and he was like, "I don't know what you were doing. If that had hit me I don't know what I would have done!"

Another time that same year, we had a curfew. Now, we don't always have one, but he had given us a curfew and apparently had notified some of the bars around town that if they saw any of us in there, they should call the basketball office and let them know.

Well, they had gotten a call from The Hawk. Brandon had been there. So the next day before practice we were all standing there and Coach Self was like, "I hope it was worth it for whoever went out. Anybody want to fess up?"

Now, Brandon is an honest guy, and he wouldn't want his teammates to have to run because he had broken curfew. "I did, Coach," he said.

Coach said, "Was it worth it?"

Brandon goes, "Yeah. It was crackin', man. It was a good time. I enjoyed it."

Coach Self laughed a little bit. You could tell he knew that was just B-Rush. He'd never lie to anybody. He would just fess up, take the punishment and go. And he was in such good shape, I don't think any amount of running would have hurt him anyway.

Many people probably remember this, but our junior year was a tough year for Cole. He was always a great player, but off the floor he had to deal with some difficult things. His grandmother, Ann, died during the season, and his dad, Walt, had lost his job. It was tough for him. We didn't talk about it a lot. It was one of those things where you were going to be there for him. Cole's a really strong person and he was able to deal with these things that were coming at him. Walt and Cathy are such great people. He has a great family back home. Blue collar people, hard-working, have worked for everything in their lives. They would do anything for you. That's the type of guy Cole is.

He is also incredibly goofy. We made a pretty good pair as roommates because he's more outgoing than I am. I'm the calm, reserved guy and he's being loud, enjoying things. He likes to be around a lot of people. We balanced each other out. He got me to be a lot more outgoing and helped me have a good time.

Cole would leave his tooth laying around.

Fortunately, he's also a pretty clean person. We also both had girlfriends throughout college, so we didn't want our place to be a dump when they would come over. The one thing he did, though, was leave his tooth laying around. He had gotten one of his teeth knocked out and had a false one. It had a retainer on it, and he would leave that thing around. He'd leave it on the bathroom sink next to my toothbrush. If he was eating, he'd leave it in the grossest spots. I was like, "Really Cole? This is what you're doing?"

He still has that thing. You'd think with a year in the NBA, it wouldn't hurt him financially to get it fixed, but I think he likes being the goof with the busted tooth. There's something about such a carefree guy who genuinely enjoys life. He couldn't care less if he wasn't a basketball player. He would enjoy whatever he was doing.

Another thing about Cole is that he thinks he's a great chef, and he actually is a pretty good cook. It always came out all right. He loves pickles, though, and he knows I hate them. So he used to come stand in my doorway eating a pickle just to annoy me. Sometimes he'd come say he wanted to play H-O-R-S-E, so we'd go into the living room, set a dollar on the table and play H-O-R-S-E on our Nerf hoop. We never had to force anything. We got along naturally. Cole will be a friend for life.

When he left for the NBA after that season, I was sad to see him go, but I knew he was ready. I had seen the progress he made. We faced each other when we were in high school, I saw him progress his freshman and sophomore years, and I knew it was time for him to fulfill his dream. There was no thought that we came in together, we should finish it together. Nothing like that. When it came time, I was fully supportive of his decision. I knew it was going to be great for him and he was ready to do it. I was happy to see him go because I knew it was going to be good for him.

And the next year, I didn't look back and wonder what it would have been like if he had been around. You don't do that. You don't wonder what would have happened if Mario had come back for his senior year or whatever. You're happy for those guys. That's everybody's dream.

Having Cole around helped us that year though, no question. You could say we looked like an NBA team. We had a true center. We had size at all the positions. We had depth. Coach Self had done a great job recruiting. We felt like we were the best team in the country.

One of the trips I remember well from that year was the trip out to UCLA. We rarely do this, but that trip we decided to go out a day earlier than usual. We went into this guy's huge house. We actually practiced there. That's how huge this place was. He had a gym. We met Jaleel White there (you might know him as Urkel from Family Matters). It was a rare chance for us to actually see the city where we were playing. Sometimes people talk to me about the cool places we've played. I'm like, yep, I saw the bus, the airplane, the hotel, and the gym. That's about it. We don't leave our rooms, really, for any reason when we're on the road. Even if you needed something like some aspirin or something, you'd just call a trainer. You aren't even supposed to go to a convenience store. So we enjoyed that trip to UCLA.

I was excited to play at Pauley Pavilion. There has been so much history there, all the national championships, John Wooden. The place wasn't quite what I was expecting. The arena was old, the locker room was small and old. I thought it would be a newer, nice arena. Don't get me wrong, it was kind of cool when you look back on it. It was a good experience, but not quite what I was expecting.

You run into the occasional celebrity as a KU basketball player. This is Jaleel White, but we also met Lil Wayne, Jason Sudeikis (Saturday Night Live) and some others during my four years.

One of the coolest places I got to play was at Madison Square Garden my senior year. It's the Mecca of basketball. That was always a dream for me. You see the Knicks play there. All the major tournaments are there. MSG is just this old building. You take these huge elevators behind the arena into the pit. You think of all the great performers – basketball players, athletes, musical artists who have made that same trip. It's cool. They have pictures of Michael Jackson, Jay-Z, Garth Brooks, everybody who has performed there. It's cool to think that you're doing the same thing. The locker rooms are really old. You kind of get that storied feel that this has been around for a long time. When you're on the court, you look into the stands and it's really dark out there. They put all the lights on the court, which kind of makes it like a stage.

While I'm at it, I will note that a slippery floor is a major pet peeve of mine. As you can see reading through this book, I really don't make a big deal out of anything. For example, some people were pretty fired up when Baylor coach Scott Drew pulled his team off the floor so they wouldn't see our pre-game introductions video. To me? Whatever. When Denis Clemente hit me in the back of the head during a game my junior year, I didn't think much of it. But I am annoyed by a slick floor.

The floor at Madison Square Garden was slippery, I think, because they had a bunch of dancers working out on it, rehearsing for something that wasn't related to basketball. I think they must have brought some dust onto the floor that didn't get cleaned off. It was one of the slicker courts I've played on.

The floors that really bugged me in the Big 12 were Bramlage Coliseum and Hilton Coliseum (at Iowa State). Trust me, I am not alone on this. I would actually talk to players about this, sometimes during games. My senior year during a game at Iowa State, I was guarding Scott Christopherson. We were standing at a free throw, and I was like, "Man, is your floor always this slick?" He goes, "Yeah, man, it's terrible." Same story at Kansas State. I've asked Pullen and some of those guys about the floor and they're like, "Yeah, dude, our floor is terrible." They don't like it either. Whenever you're watching a game on TV and you see a couple opposing players talking to each other, it's probably going to be something like that as opposed to what people think of as "trash talking."

The floor aside, though, I did enjoy playing in both of those arenas. Hilton was old and kind of cool. It seats a ton of people, and they always played us tough up there (even though we didn't lose there in my four years). I would say Bramlage was the best road atmosphere I've played in. Whenever we played there, they were always amped to play us. Fans showed up early and had creative signs. It was genuinely a loud arena to play in. They put the fans almost literally right on the floor, too. When you're inbounding a ball, you could sit down in their laps. Because they're so close, you can hear all the stuff they say to you. Most of the time they aren't saying much, but you kind of enjoy it when they do. You like when people start saying stuff. It makes it fun. You feel like you are the opponent in this place and people are against you. It's always more fun to beat somebody on their floor because you feel like you're taking something away from them.

The thing everybody saw was Clemente hitting me in the back of the head.

My junior year, we did just that in Manhattan. We beat K-State three times that year, including in the Big 12 Tournament championship game, but the game in Manhattan was easily the most talked about. What turned it from a regular rivalry game to a supposed controversy was a moment everybody saw and a moment only one person supposedly heard. The thing everybody saw was Clemente hitting me in the back of the head. I had gone to box him out on a free throw. I didn't feel like I boxed him out overly hard, but I guess he wasn't expecting it. So he popped me in the head. I think he just got caught up in the moment. I must have a hard head, because it didn't really faze me.

K-State suspended him one game for doing that. But their next game was against North Carolina Central, so it didn't even matter. They won easily. The next time we played, he came over and said, "Man, my bad." I told him not to worry about it. That's just not the kind of thing I spend much time getting worked up over. I'm not too dramatic.

The other thing that kept people talking about that game long after it was over was that I guess somebody said they heard someone on or near our bench yell something to Clemente about a green card. I don't really know what that was about. Nobody on our team would have said that. Like I said, we know those guys personally. We work camps together in the offseason. I get that fans might despise each other, but it isn't that way for us players. I don't know if something got lost in translation or maybe somebody took something differently than it was meant. Granted, it is a rivalry, we're all college kids and we might say some things we don't really mean. But there would have been nothing said like that.

That was a close, intense game. Sherron made some huge plays late, and we won in overtime. It pushed our record to 20-1 and 6-0 in the Big 12. K-State was ranked 11th. It was a big win, a road win. We wouldn't be facing a tougher environment the rest of the season, and we had gone in there and won.

That was on a Saturday. Wednesday night, we went to overtime at Colorado but won that one, too. We didn't lose again until, go figure, we played at Oklahoma State, which was our third-to-last game of the regular season. We finished off the conference season beating both of our rivals, won the title with a 14-2 record, and won the Big 12 tournament.

So it was off to Oklahoma City to play Lehigh in the first round of the NCAA Tournament. I know it has never happened before, but a No. 16 seed is going to beat a No. 1 one of these years. It's inevitable. Those teams are good enough that in those weird arenas with the weird crowds, they could start making shots and there you go. I'm telling you, this is going to happen at some point.

You could see how it was within the realm of possibility by watching our first half against Lehigh. They had a lead for a while and it was still a close game at halftime. I think we came out a little tight that game. Shots weren't falling. When shots aren't falling, you resort to forcing things you shouldn't. I'm not saying we did that, but in general that's what happens. We didn't play that well. Give Lehigh credit for scouting us well. But we played better in the second half and pulled away, meaning in the second round we were facing Northern Iowa, which had won a close game over UNLV.

The scouting report was basically this:

We knew they were a possession team. They were an opportunistic running team. They wouldn't take a shot early in the shot clock. They were going to move it to get the shot they wanted. You've got to be sound defensively against a team like that. That was going to be the key for us.

The whole game, Northern Iowa played really well. They played to the scouting report they had on us. They didn't waste possessions. They had some good players who played well. Their big guy (Jordan Eglseder) wasn't known for knocking down threes and he hits two on us. It's one of those games I'm sure they felt like they had nothing to lose. That's a good feeling to have as a team. When nobody is going to say anything to you when you lose or get blown out, that's an easy way to play.

One thing you don't want to give a team is confidence to think they can hang with you. By not playing well in the first half, I think we gave them that feeling that they were going to be in the game and control the tempo.

We had to start pressing, and it worked. Sherron had made a couple of free throws to make it a one-point game in the final minute. We set up our press and almost got a steal. But they broke it.

Sherron was running back on defense and Ali Farokhmanesh had the ball. I didn't know if Sherron was going to take the ball or the basket. I was kind of at the basket. Ali is dribbling up, and I'm thinking he's going to pull it back out and reset their offense, which is how they always played. I waited for Sherron to get back to the basket. Usually stopping the ball is the most important thing – I just didn't think he would pull a three at that moment. I backed off a little. In hindsight it was a bad move on my part, but knowing what I knew at the time, I really did not think he was going to shoot it. I probably should have been up close to him to give him that feeling he shouldn't have shot it, but at the moment I didn't think it was bad to be backed off because the way they had been playing was so conservative. They were making sure they got a good shot each time. That was probably the earliest they shot in the shot clock the entire game and that was with 35 seconds left.

You make that shot, you become the hero. He did it.

If you lose in that first weekend you feel like you were never in the tournament. That's how it felt. We never felt like we were in it. It was sad.

It's a terrible feeling to know you had a great season and set yourself up to make a big run in the tournament. We didn't overlook Northern Iowa. I don't think we ever overlooked an opponent. We knew all about what had happened against Bucknell and Bradley. Northern Iowa just plain outplayed us that day. If you lose in that first weekend you feel like you were never in the tournament. That's how it felt. We never felt like we were in it. It was sad.

I think we were definitely in the conversation for winning the national championship that year. We had the pieces at every position. We had weapons. All my four years I felt like we had an opportunity to win the national championship. It just wasn't our year.

An unusual thing about that year was that we probably played our best game in January, against Temple. It was the perfect mix of everybody clicking on the same day. It doesn't often happen that everybody plays their best on the same day, and most of the teams I've played on had their best games later in the year. Maybe that was Northern Iowa's game where they had everybody clicking.

—◆—

A couple of years removed from it, having played in the NBA, Aldrich has a fresh perspective on that team.

"I don't know if it was that we peaked a little early as a team," he said. "You kind of look at it, at least from my perspective with the NBA playoffs, you look at the (2010-11) San Antonio Spurs, a team that played so well during the regular season, were leading the league for just about the whole season, then you get to the playoffs and they kind of fell apart because they peaked early.

"I don't know if going through the whole season we were thinking that we've lost two games all season, and then going into the tournament people are just going to roll over for us. It just didn't happen that way. My freshman year we had that killer mentality. We're going to beat you guys by 50. I don't think that team our junior year had that. I think that was hard because guys who have been around, guys like Sherron and Tyrel and Brady and myself, knew how to have that killer mentality, but we just didn't have it. That was one of the things that nipped us at the end. We could have beaten a team by 15 or 17, but we were complacent with beating them by nine."

—◆—

We, of course, knew that team was over. Sherron was a senior and I had a good feeling Cole and Xavier were going to the NBA. You always look back and say your "what-ifs" right after the season. Man, if a few things would have changed. That was a tough loss to get over for all of us. You never want a senior to go out like that. But you can't dwell on that. You can't long for how things would be different if guys came back the next year. We had a great team. We had our opportunity. It just didn't work out.

The great thing was – and the great thing about playing at Kansas is – we had another great team coming back the next year.

Sweaty Feet

Larry Hare is our equipment manager and he has a lot of experience with athletic equipment. He worked at UConn, Boston College, Northern Arizona. He's been doing this since the mid-1990s.

Larry says I have the sweatiest feet he's ever seen. I routinely destroy basketball shoes with my sweat. I can wring dripping sweat out of my socks after a practice. I can't wear the same pair of shoes two days in a row, because that doesn't allow them enough time to dry out. During the season, I blow through a pair of basketball shoes every three weeks, because the sweat wears them out.

Which isn't a problem. We have a contract with Adidas, of course, and we can get as many replacement pairs as necessary. Anyway, during the Cal game my senior year – incidentally, probably my best game in college – I blew out an almost brand-new pair during the game. The sole separated from the boot, so for part of a play I was running around, essentially, in a sweaty sock. Fortunately, there was a TV timeout soon, so a trainer ran back and got me a new pair. I didn't end up missing any game action because of it.

So I don't know if anybody ever noticed it, but I wore a lot of different shoes over the course of my career. Actually, I have way too many shoes at my house. Probably more than 100 pairs of shoes.

A lot of basketball players have really nasty feet.

This is partially because I just love shoes. But it's also because basketball is really hard on your feet. I don't want anybody seeing my gnarly toes. A lot of basketball players have really nasty feet. Thomas Robinson has this bad hammer toe. Cole does, too. Mario Little has really ugly feet. In the summertime, all my friends will be wearing flip flops. I'm going with Vans or something. Nobody is seeing these things.

8:00 April 8, 2009

Dear Tyrel,
I Like your basketball games. Even if your team loses I am still proud of the Jayhawks. My teacher is crazy about watching your games. She always puts your show on even if she has work to do. I will not stop watching it until it's over. I wonder if you'll be on tomorrow. I hope you like the supply my class put in the fun box for you. Your coach is awesome!
Your fan,
Madelyn

We get great stuff to wear from Adidas. There are a lot of jumpsuits, which we would wear traveling to and from games. Coach Manning is really big on presentation. We would wear one jump suit to the game, and wear a different one after it. But we'd always all be dressed alike.

But anyway, there's some info about my feet. You're welcome.

Our coaches do a terrific job of drawing up plays during timeouts.

Nothing gets the crowd going like an alley-oop.

We have won seven of these in a row. Our philosophy is that if you win the Big 12 championship, you're in the conversation to win the national championship.

(Above) One of the bigger shots I made in my career came in a game against Nebraska, which also had a Kansas kid: Caleb Walker (25), who is from Hutchinson.

(Left) Playing in front of a packed house every night was awesome ... even when you did get taken out.

Defense was always something I felt I needed to work on, especially earlier in my career. I never expected to be blocking a lot of shots, though.

(Inset) Our fans are awesome. I can honestly say I never got tired of signing autographs or talking to fans or taking pictures with people. It's one of the coolest things about being a player at Kansas.

I don't know whether I made or missed this shot, but one thing about my stroke is that it has always been a little flat. That's just the way it worked for me, I guess.

Sometimes people say the Fieldhouse doesn't hurt the other team, it only helps us. Maybe that's' true, but I think some teams can get intimidated by it all.

I had the highest vertical on the team. Here's one way to work on it: Put 135 pounds on your shoulders and jump.

*I know KU and K-State fans don't get along real well, and we do play some intense games
with the Wildcats, but the truth is that I was always friends with most of those guys.*

Two of the funniest guys I ever played with are in this photo.
It was cool Brady Morningstar and Mario Little who got to show the fans their
personalities on senior night. Thomas Robinson (left) is known to crack a joke too.

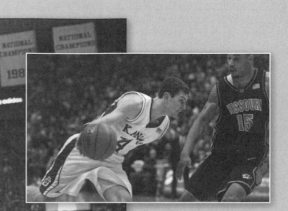

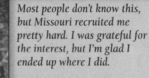

Most people don't know this, but Missouri recruited me pretty hard. I was grateful for the interest, but I'm glad I ended up where I did.

A lot of times, players from schools like Emporia State will talk about how cool it is to play in the Fieldhouse. Even for an exhibition game, the place is packed.

At first, I didn't know if I wanted my sister, Lacie, around all the time. But she was a manager for three of my years, and I wouldn't change a thing.

*Will Spradling (55), is from a much bigger town than Burlington,
but as a fellow Kansan he knows all about this rivalry.*

Holding a trophy never gets old. Between the regular season and Big 12 tournament, we took home seven of these in my time at KU.

I don't remember this play, but if you want to believe I blocked this shot, by all means, go ahead.

Your whole life, you watch the "One Shining Moment" video at the end of the NCAA Tournament. What you may not realize is that they play that video in the arena after the game. We all got to watch it.

The great thing about being a classmate of a 6'11" guy is that everybody is watching him.

*The twins were some of the
smartest players I played with,
and great teammates, too.
We still keep in touch.*

(Above) I am so blessed to have parents who were so supportive of me my whole life. There were a lot of sacrifices for both of them and it was awesome to have them recognized on the court before the game.

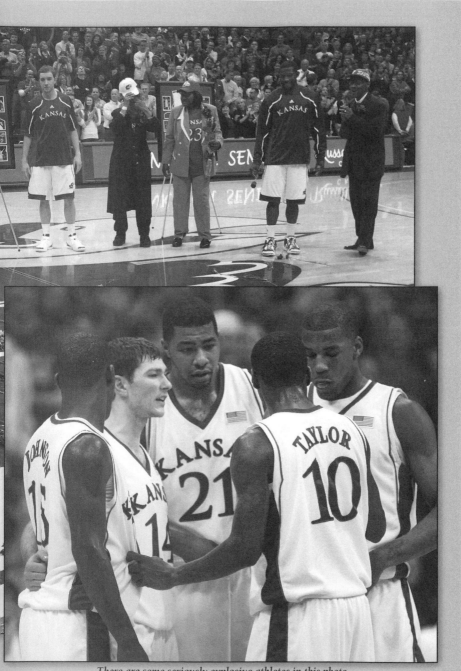

There are some seriously explosive athletes in this photo.

Not that I have already obtained all this, or have already arrived at my goal, but I press on to take hold of that for which Christ Jesus took hold of me.[13] Brothers and sisters, I do not consider myself yet to have taken hold of it. But one thing I do: Forgetting what is behind and straining toward what is ahead,[14] I press on toward the goal to win the prize for which God has called me heavenward in Christ Jesus.

James 1:2

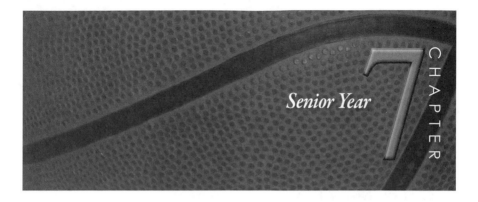

Senior Year

We players get four tickets to every home game. Some of us use all of them each time. It was always easy for me. My parents, my sister, and my then-girlfriend got my four tickets. But some players who are from far away might not need all of theirs. For example, Elijah Johnson, who is from Las Vegas, might need to give out only two of his tickets. So what he'll do is enter them into a Web site we have so that anybody else on the team can get those tickets if they need them. You have to say how many you're taking, who is using them and what their relationship is to you. All those tickets are in a section a few rows behind the visiting team's bench. That's where all the players' families sit.

You've probably heard about the ticket scandal that erupted at KU in 2009. It is sad that happened with a lot of tickets. There are people out there who pay good money to sit in good seats. It's sad to have those going to ticket brokers or people who otherwise weren't paying for them in the right way, people making money off it. It's sad when you see people taking advantage of something like that.

That ticket issue blew up during the summer before my senior year. Our athletic director, Lew Perkins, ended up retiring soon after that, which was too bad. I really liked Lew and what he did for Kansas athletics. I like our new AD, Sheahon Zenger, as well. But the whole ticket problem was sad.

As you might imagine, it didn't really affect us as a basketball team. You don't like seeing that happen at a school you love, but it's not like it has anything to do with running in boot camp, paying attention to the scouting report, or guarding Jordan Hamilton.

Kind of like with the football-basketball conflict from the year before, I think the start of the football season and then the basketball season helped take people's minds off that stuff.

Even though we had lost three really good players, three guys who all ended up on NBA rosters, I knew we had a really good team coming back. Like I said, you could make a strong argument Marcus had been our best player for a good stretch of his sophomore year. Markieff was better than most people realized at the time. We had experience and we got Josh Selby, a super-talented freshman. It seems like it always goes that way. Guys leave, and new guys come in, returning players get better. The beat goes on.

I never really looked down the road or looked at the big picture, but I knew that if we took it one step at a time, Coach Self would get us to the point where we were in position to contend for it all by the end of the year.

Our first really good win was in Las Vegas against Arizona. I don't think most people knew it at the time, but Derrick Williams is a fabulous talent. He was a tough matchup with an inside-outside game. He has a great body and has that same knack for the ball that Cole had. I'm not surprised he ended up being the second pick in the NBA draft. As you could see by their tournament run, they had a really good team that year. We also had a nice win against Ohio out there.

I know I have made this point already, but the answer is no, we didn't do anything in Vegas. Bus, plane, bus, hotel room, arena, bus, hotel room, bus, arena, bus, plane. That's it. Those games are played at The Orleans Arena, which is literally attached to a casino. They also host hockey games and I don't know what else there. I'm told the basketball court actually sits on top of the ice hockey rink, but you couldn't tell. The only weird thing was that the floor had some dead spots in it, where the ball didn't bounce normally.

Speaking of the ball, it is another thing that is a bit of a pet peeve of mine. In college basketball, you don't play with the same ball every game. It has to do with coaches' contracts with these different manufacturers, but there is a Nike ball, an Adidas ball, a Wilson ball, a ball called The Rock. And they all feel a little different. The grooves are different. I know they're all the same weight, but the Wilson one feels heavier, and I like that about it. That's the one we use at our home games and it's the same one they use in the NCAA Tournament. A lot of the Big 12 schools – Texas, Iowa State, Kansas State, Colorado, Oklahoma, Oklahoma State, Missouri – use the Nike ball, which I got used to. Texas Tech uses some weird Mizuno ball, which sucks. Nebraska uses the Adidas ball, which I still don't like. We played with The Rock at Madison Square Garden. I think that's an East Coast thing.

This may seem like a little thing, but as a shooter, you'd really like it to be uniform. In the NBA, they play with the same ball every night. In college, you may play with the Nike ball on Monday, then come home and play with the Wilson ball Saturday, then play with the Adidas ball Wednesday. I found that to be kind of annoying.

I felt bad for Josh during this part of the year, because he was suspended by the NCAA for accepting improper benefits when he was in junior high. The NCAA has its rules and I know those are in place for a reason. It was too bad he couldn't play those games.

Being a freshman is difficult enough, but he had to deal with all that on top of it. Plus, he had broken his finger over the summer. Then when school started, he could practice, then he wasn't allowed to practice. It was an extremely tough situation for Josh.

I know it was rough on him and draining and taxing on him mentally and physically. He had to deal with a lot of things on and off the court most players don't have to. With us guys he always had a good attitude. You can understand why he'd be down at times. Who wouldn't be? Overall he handled it great. I loved Josh as a teammate. When he hurt his foot he saw a specialist in North Carolina. I flew out there with him because they wanted to check out my foot as well. We went to North Carolina together. I got to know him on that trip. It was just me, him, and our trainer. It was a time for us to grow closer together. I really respect Josh as a player and all the things he went through.

People compared his personality to Sherron's a lot, and I can see that. They both hate to lose. Sherron had the ability to change the mood of a room and control everyone else that I don't think Josh had quite yet. But they both came from tough backgrounds and had tough lives and made the most of their time in college.

It's hard enough for a freshman, but Josh Selby had a lot of tough breaks on top of it.

Josh is a great player. He's extremely athletic. I think he's going to do great in the NBA. It probably didn't go the way he wanted to, getting drafted in the second round. But he is extremely athletic, is a great shooter and understands the game well. It was just an awkward situation where maybe if there wasn't the one-and-done rule he would have gone out of high school and things would have been different for him.

His first game was against USC in the Fieldhouse. He came off the bench, scored 21 points and made the game-winning shot. I can't imagine a debut game going any better. I knew he had that ability. You just never know how somebody is going to react when they get out there that first time on that big of a stage. You don't want to judge somebody's career on one game. People probably expected he'd play that way every game. That's not fair to him being so young and having to deal with the things he did.

It seemed like whenever he was starting to find his niche, something would happen and he couldn't get comfortable. That's gotta be tough as a freshman. It's tough for anybody. I wouldn't say he was bumming, though. He had the team in mind. Things hadn't gone his way, so you could understand where he was coming from. He definitely was in it for us. He encouraged his teammates. I have nothing but good things to say about Josh.

He played a nice game at Cal, which was where I had the best game of my career, at least from a statistical perspective. I had 18 points and seven rebounds and made most of my shots. We won the game in front of a crowd that had to be half KU fans. It was amazing. After it was over, I walked over to the sideline and raised a couple thumbs up to the KU fans for supporting us. Some Cal people booed. I didn't mean any disrespect by it. I was just thanking our fans for being so good. It's amazing how many KU fans show up at road arenas all around the country.

That game was on December 22, right before Christmas break. Unfortunately, I sustained a foot injury during Christmas break that would hound me the rest of the season.

There are some oddities about my feet. One of them is that the amount of sweat that comes out of them is literally enough to routinely destroy a pair of basketball shoes in a matter of weeks. Another is that I actually have an extra bone in my ankle. I have what is called the os trigonum, which is an extra bone that no more than 8 percent of people have. You can get something called os trigonum syndrome, which usually happens to people who put a lot of stress on their feet. It's not uncommon for ballet dancers to get it.

I had tweaked my ankle, which had caused this bone to start rubbing against different tendons and ligaments, just making everything inflamed. It was pretty painful, yet it was kind of a day-by-day thing. Some mornings it would feel absolutely terrible. I felt like I could barely walk on it. Some days it would feel a lot better. It really started hurting me the Texas Tech game and I didn't play that much.

This is something that can be fixed with surgery, and I did have surgery on it after the season, but we had no way of knowing exactly how long I would have been out. It could have been three weeks, or it could have been three months. Everybody responds to it differently. We didn't want to risk it being a season-ending surgery, so the only alternative was to play on it and take some pain killers.

—◆—

As tough as Self knew Tyrel was, he could tell by the end of the season there was only so much Tyrel's body was capable of doing.

"People don't know, but he only practiced the day before games," Self said. It was bad enough they removed a piece of bone a week after our season was over and it was far larger than we even thought it was going into it. It hurt him basically the whole year. The last half it became a major issue. At the end, it continually got worse and worse and worse to where he was probably playing at about 80 percent or 75 percent of what he was. It was amazing, after he had surgery, three weeks later he was back to 100 percent. We just didn't have an opportunity to do the surgery during the season.

—◆—

From the Texas Tech game on, I got a shot in my butt before every game to stem the pain. I got a couple cortisone shots, too. They would shoot cortisone directly into my heel. That sucked. It was a long needle and they'd stick it in near your Achilles. I'm kind of a wimp, and not a fan of needles.

But even with the shot in the butt and the shot in the ankle, I wasn't playing pain free. The most difficult thing was getting warmed up. It was painful to start practice and go through the drills to get going. Once I got a sweat going I could loosen it up and make it feel better. I remember it being tough during shootarounds or before the games. Once the game started your adrenaline kicked in and it got a little bit easier, although it was always a bit nagging. You felt like you were a step slower. I couldn't jump that great off that foot. I tried to jump off two feet when I could. I don't want to sound like a hero, here. There are people who deal with way worse things than that, but it did affect me. I'm not sure it ever affected my shooting mechanics, but I did try to avoid pivoting off my left foot whenever possible. When I was coming off screens, I'd try to make sure the pivot was off my right foot.

It was bad enough that it kept me out of practice. I could do some things, but I spent a lot of time on the stationary bike, trying to keep my wind up (breathing capacity). You can lose that quickly if you don't practice every day.

It really bugged me that I couldn't be out there practicing with my teammates. I had hardly ever missed a practice before that and I could see them out there, tired, needing a sub, and I couldn't do anything. Sometimes the coaches would give me a hard time, like, "Oh, here he is on the sideline. Are they paying you to coach?"

I really respected my teammates for being cool with it. They could have resented me for that. I wasn't practicing, but I was still getting to start and play. The Lord truly helped me get through this time and I look at Him as the only reason I was able to keep playing throughout the season.

It has been pointed out to me that I was the only guy on our team who started every game that year. I feel blessed that I got to do that, but that distinction doesn't really mean much to me. There's no reason other guys wouldn't have started every game if some things hadn't happened. It's not like the twins weren't good enough to start all 38 games or something. I don't look at is as a great accomplishment. I was lucky coach kept playing me. He could have chosen not to play me when I was hurt.

Hopefully in a few years I'll have another graduation, this time from medical school. I doubt I'll be posing with Mario Little and Coach Self after that one, though.

Looking back on it, it's cool how my career went exactly the way Coach Self told me it would when he was recruiting me. I feel like I was truly blessed by the Lord for my career to go the way it did. I was on a national championship team, and nobody can ever take that away. We won four Big 12 regular season championships. All those things I'm extremely proud of. There's nothing I would change or do differently. I'm completely happy with the way it went. You wish we would have won more games and not lost certain ones, but you can't go back and change anything. That shows you how honest Coach Self will be with you in recruiting. He said you come here and work hard, things will work out for you. That's the way it went.

Even though I was battling my injury and Josh was still trying to get comfortable, things were going great. We finished the nonconference season undefeated and won our first three Big 12 games.

We were getting ready to play Texas in another one of those big games against UT. It was well after curfew when I got a text from Mario saying Thomas Robinson's mom had died. Curfew was 10:30 p.m. He called me about midnight to say a bunch of them were at Thomas' and Elijah's room. We knew this was one of those situations when curfew didn't matter. Everybody gathered there.

To see the sadness in the room … there's no way you can feel bad enough for somebody who's going through that. After losing his grandparents and losing his mom, you can imagine how completely crushed he would be. He stayed at Angel Morris' house that night because they wanted to make sure somebody was around him all night. I can't imagine he got a wink of sleep. Angel was there in the room, Tyshawn's mom was there, Coach Self was there, Coach Dooley was there. We all sat together in the living room. Nobody said much. Before everyone left, Angel asked me to say a prayer for everyone. We were huddled together, holding hands, saying a prayer as a team. It was a heartfelt moment. God was in control of the whole situation. We know we're not in control and there's a greater cause and his mom's in a better place.

Thomas played in the game the next day.

Think about that. He played in the game. I don't know how. I don't know how he could muster enough energy and enough courage to do that. It's crazy. Thomas Robinson is the toughest kid I've ever known.

We lost the game and it ended our winning streak in the Fieldhouse. I suppose fatigue, emotional and physical, could have been a part of it, but athletes can't look at things that way. They weren't going to cancel the game, so we had to perform. It was probably the most emotional game I've been a part of.

We had a really rough night before that game, but they weren't going to cancel the game. You have to perform.

There isn't any excuse for losing. I want people to know that. Regardless of what happened, you've got to play the game. But certainly people were just a little drained mentally and physically. That's the one time we came in the locker room after the game and as upset as people were at the loss, you look back and see that Coach handled this tragedy the best way a coach could handle it. Ending the streak, losing to Texas … it didn't seem that bad. This was a life thing, not a basketball thing.

It didn't end there for Thomas, either. He had to make funeral arrangements for his mom. He had to go through her stuff and decide who got what and what went there. He had to be there for his sister, Jayla, who was 9 years old at the time. He missed the game at Colorado. I'm so proud of how he's handled all this. He has handled it as well as anybody could.

That loss put us behind Texas in the Big 12 race. As usual, the Longhorns had a great team and we knew there was little margin for error if we were going to win our seventh consecutive title. We won a close game at Colorado, then went on a tear, setting up another big game against K-State in Manhattan.

Jacob Pullen scored 38 and they ran away with it. You never want a great player like that to get confident. Because here's what happens with a player like him: He makes a few good looks, and so he starts taking some bad looks, then the bad looks start going down, and you're in trouble. There's not much you can do when a guy is knocking down tough, guarded looks. Pullen knocked down everything that night. I always loved playing at Bramlage and at Missouri, but this was K-State's night.

Bramlage is a tough place to play, and we have an intense rivalry, but I have to say I am as entertained by watching Frank Martin as anybody. He's extremely passionate. Those guys love playing for him. They say it's a transition learning how to cope with him, but he's always going to be on your side, go to bat for you no matter what. I do think it's weird they call him Frank. I feel like you call your coach Coach. I don't understand that part. Even if I met him, which I have, I'd call him Coach Martin, even though he isn't my coach. I wouldn't call him Frank. I've never called Coach Self "Bill" and I never will. He's Coach Self. Even my high school coaches and middle school coaches are Coach to me, with one exception: I don't call my dad "Coach." I call him Dad.

That was our last loss of the Big 12 season and we went into Senior Night with the league title wrapped up. Texas had lost three times, so a win on Senior Night guaranteed us at least a share of the Big 12 title and a win in Columbia would give it to us outright.

On Senior Night, you still get only your four allotted tickets, but Coach Self is good about making sure the seniors get what they need. Basically, if you aren't a senior, you only give out the bare minimum of your allotment so the seniors can invite extra people.

I don't think there are many other places in the country where fans would sit around for an hour after the game is over to watch basketball players speak, and that's one of the things that makes it special to play there. The place will be full to the rafters for senior speeches. Because of all the hoopla, it feels like that night is about the seniors, but it really isn't. It's really about everybody else. Everybody who has been there for you along the way. All your teammates. The fans. It's your chance to thank everybody for making it so special.

That's what I wanted to express on Senior Night. I wasn't nervous to speak in front of everybody, although Brady and Mario were tough acts to follow. Those guys are both really funny. Brady made a joke about he and Coach Self being the same age. People got to see his personality a little bit. I forgot to thank my teammates, but they made sure I did at the end.

It is rare for a KU senior to make it through Senior Night without tearing up.

As far as I'm concerned, Senior Night isn't about the seniors, it's about everybody else.

I just want to say how thankful I am for the fans. I've played at places around the country, and there's not a better place to play. I don't care what people say about Cameron Indoor Stadium at Duke or Rupp Arena at Kentucky or whatever. Those places may be good and all, but I doubt there's a place that's as intimate but as large with as much tradition as Kansas.

There's a special feeling in there and a special sound. Sometimes there are these moments in games where – and I don't know how to put my finger on it – you can just feel something change. You can feel the crowd change. There's an urgency that washes over the place. You can tell what the crowd is feeling. They spur you on. Maybe it's a tight game and the crowd can sense something. Then you sense the crowd sensing something. For example, my senior year when we were playing Nebraska, it was a tight game. We had gotten down by double digits but had cut it to four midway through the second half. You could just feel something was about to happen. Well, Tyshawn missed a layup and Markieff went to save it as it was headed out of bounds. He flung it backward, and Brady had to save it back to Markieff, who swung it to the opposite wing to me for a big three. Fieldhouse magic.

You just sort of know when it's time for a big shot, so you know when you've hit one. I'm not one to go crazy and throw up the three goggles or do anything cool with my hands. I'm not smart enough to think on the fly. I don't know how those guys do it. I might pump my fist or something. It's the crowd that gets you going, really. When you hit a big one, it's almost like the crowd pushed you to making that big shot. You just know when the time is right.

I still get goosebumps in that place. My skin literally tightens up. It happens when I run out of the tunnel before games. It's kind of dark in the tunnel, and as you look down it, you can't really see much of the arena. Just part of the floor, some ushers, maybe a few fans. You jog out and all the sudden … boom! The bright lights, the roar, the band. It all comes splashing down on you. There's such a feeling to it. There's such an aura. It is impossible to forget where you are and everything that has happened there.

I still get goosebumps at Allen Fieldhouse.

When they start playing the national anthem, that's when I feel like it's game time. I always say a prayer during the anthem. I look up at the flag, say a prayer and think about how fortunate I am to be there.

Not many kids have gotten that opportunity.

Coach Self has said before that he thinks the home crowd helps the home team but doesn't hurt the visiting team. But I can see how a visiting team could get overwhelmed by it all. On the other hand, I can see where some players would feed off it, wanting to shut everybody up.

I'm that way. As fun as it is to make a big shot at home, I loved making a big one on the road. It happened at Missouri my senior year, the final regular-season game of the year. We were up pretty good but MU was making a late comeback. We were up by four with 1:33 left, and we ran a version of "chop," the same play we ran to get Mario the ball in the national title game. Only this time, I was open, Tyshawn found me, and I knocked it down in front of the Missouri student section. We're up seven now, and the crowd knows it's over. You live for moments like that. There's nothing they can do, nothing they can say. It's over.

There's a photo of me right after I made that shot looking into the student section and yelling. A lot of people like that photo, I think, because it looks like I'm jawing at the Mizzou kids. I wasn't saying anything, just letting it out.

That sealed the outright conference championship, which was nice. You don't like sharing those. And, as we've established, conference championships are really important to us at Kansas.

But we still had some work to do in order to make sure we were in the best position possible heading into the NCAA Tournament. Besides, we like winning Big 12 Tournament trophies, too.

We got to the championship game for a rematch with Texas. We were pumped. They were pumped. It was going to be a great game.

Now, in the grand scheme, this is a pretty small thing, but at this point I had never dunked in a college game. I had dunked a lot in high school and I dunked all the time in practice, but for a combination of reasons had never done it in a game. A lot of times you're already so tired from playing defense that you just don't have the energy, so you lay it up.

Plus, my bum wheel was my left ankle. The left foot is the main jumping foot for a right-handed player and that thing was painful for me. Well, I got a runout against Texas and for some reason I decided to go for it. I finally got my dunk. That's one of the games that immediately sticks out to me when I think about my career.

We were playing great basketball at that point. I really felt like we were peaking. Sure, I wish my ankle hadn't been hurt and Josh was completely healthy, but heading into the tournament we were confident.

I don't think anybody on my team was a thug. But it is true that some people started to see us that way. This happened because of a couple incidents. Another factor was that the twins always got lumped together. Everybody does it, because they are so similar, but what that meant was that if one of them did something, it was perceived that both of them did something. And they did get called for some elbows throughout the season. When you do that, people are going to be on the watch even more, to the point that they might not be doing anything three other guys on the floor are doing, but they get noticed because they're the ones everybody is watching. In reality, they're the nicest kids ever. It was unfair the way they were labeled.

So there was this perception, and then we had that little dust-up in the tunnel before the Richmond game. Let me explain what that was all about. You're supposed to run out at different times so you don't meet each other. They ran out first and had stopped in the middle of the tunnel and circled up, doing a dance or something. That's what teams do. That's fine. But we needed a way to get out there, too, so we weren't going to let them stand in front of us. So we barged through. It became a shoving match. I think everything could have been avoided if they had done their huddle out on the court. I don't know who is in charge of the timing of all that, but the next time they made sure that didn't happen. They made sure everyone was clear by the time you ran out of there. It was a bunch of testosterone-filled guys. They're in our way and we're going to go through them.

The other thing that happened was, within range of some TV cameras, Marcus told some Richmond guys they'd better be ready. He had done something similar before we played Texas in the Big 12 championship game. It wasn't a big deal. Personally, it's not something I would do. I would rather just let our play do the talking, but it didn't bother me that he did this. It's just the way he was raised to play. It is neither good nor bad. Those guys just like to talk. I think it was blown out of proportion.

We beat Richmond, which put is in the Elite Eight, facing a No. 11 seed in VCU. As I said, we don't overlook anybody. We have never done that, and we didn't overlook VCU.

We just couldn't make shots.

We were the best shooting team in the nation in 2010-11, but couldn't get any shots to fall against VCU.

I guess people probably wonder about the effect my ankle had on my shooting. I went 1-for-9 from the field and 1-for-7 from the three-point line. The thing is, I had been making shots other times, so I don't see any reason I shouldn't have made them that game. I just didn't. I don't think you can blame it on the ankle. For whatever reason, none of us shot well that day. Except for Tyshawn. He was the only guy on our team who made at least half his shots. We shot 36 percent. VCU made 12 threes. We lost by 10.

— ◆ —

From the stands, Debbie Reed felt the same thing every Kansas fan felt.

"He liked to be the game-changer," she said. "That last game he played I kept waiting for it to happen. Tyrel's gonna hit a shot, Tyrel's gonna hit a shot that's going to change everything. It just didn't happen for him that game. You wonder if, with all that ball-playing that weekend, was that ankle just getting to where he couldn't get his shot off the way he used to? You can't second-guess that, either."

Tyrel's roommate, Curt Welter, says that such a shooting night shows how difficult it is to make a shot in a Division I basketball game.

Welter would sometimes go with Tyrel when he went to the gym for extra shooting, and he has seen his roommate put on some incredible shooting exhibitions.

"There were a couple days he shot 100 threes," he said. "Not just set shooting. He would be running around. He made like 82 of them multiple times. I've never seen anything like it. It wasn't just that one day, either. He would make almost all of them. You would think that's not possible, but he dang near does."

It's a terrible feeling. You worked so hard to put yourself in the best position possible. You accomplished your biggest goal during the regular season. You knew your team was good enough to win the national championship. And it just didn't happen.

—◆—

Welter said the days following that game were the lowest he's ever seen Tyrel.

"It was tough, being his senior year," Welter said. "He had a great season, a great career. It was one of those games. Nine out of 10 times you'd put your bets on KU. That was probably the most down I've seen him, after that one."

Tyrel didn't show much, but Welter could tell.

"He's not angry at anybody, he'll kind of just shut himself off," he said. "Rather than coming home and sitting around and talking to us, having a good time, he'll want time to himself. He'll head up to his room. I'd always try to get him to do something else. He was constantly thinking about it because he wanted it so bad. Usually after a day or two he was back to being himself. There was always a time in there he would come home and not have a whole lot to say. I'd always shoot him a text after the game. You could tell even by his text back that he was hurting. He wanted to win so bad, for the fans and everybody else.

—◆—

It shows you how difficult it is to win a national title. It's weird, because you look at it, and it's just six games. Just win six games in a row. We do that all the time. But it's different. The teams are better. There are no bad teams in the NCAA Tournament, and there are plenty of great ones.

I was lucky enough to win the national championship as a freshman, then experience the heartbreak all but one team feels every year after that. That's what makes winning it so special.

GO! KU!

Dear Tyrel Reed,

My name is Marshall and go to 3rd grade at Nike Elementary. I love KU! I'm a big Jayhawk fan! My teacher is also a big fan! KU is her favorite team. I know you guys can beat North Carolina. Good luck this weekend! I know you can do it!

Sincerely,
Marshall

Sicerely,
Marshall

JWoosh

GO! KU!

"Whatever you do, work at it with all your heart, as working for the Lord, not for men."

Colossians 3:23

Off the Court

CHAPTER 8

I recently shattered the controller on my PlayStation 3.

I was playing FIFA with my roommate, Curt, and we were tied 2-2. "I'm going to score in the 90th minute," he declared. He got a runout. You know what I was saying before about how KU fans probably feel like other teams always make shots against us they would never make against other teams? Well, I knew he was going to score. I just knew it. Before he even kicked it, I raised my controller above my head and chucked it. Triangle, Square, Circle, X and Y went spraying all across my room.

Losing is the worst thing ever.

—◆—

"I've never seen a controller more broken," Welter said. "He put some power into that. I've never seen a controller snap the way it did. Every single button flew out. He was like, 'I didn't like that controller anyway.'"

—◆—

It wasn't until my sophomore year in college that I really started playing video games. In high school, I would go over to friends' houses and play, but I never even had a system until after I got out of college. This was partially because, with so many people around me who had them, I didn't need one, but also because I didn't want video games to become a big part of my life.

In high school, my friends and I would play Halo, and there is nothing that brings out the animal rage in people like that game. Sometimes it's a little embarrassing how furious you can get. I got kicked out of my friend's house a few times. In college, though, the game was Call of Duty. I love that game. Pretty good at it, too. It's the same thing with Call of Duty and FIFA as it is with Halo. I absolutely can't stand to lose. When I lose to Curt, I hate him. I will go to my room. I don't want to see him. I don't want to talk to him. I'm done with him for a while.

I'm also a golfer, and I've gotten pretty good at it. I have shot 77 twice in my life, but I usually shoot mid-80s or low 80s. That's the game I play against my dad. We golf all the time and we're very competitive with it. I get pretty mad about golf, too. I shot a 95 in June and I was so mad I put away my clubs for almost a month. I usually play once a week in the summer. I'll play at Alvamar or Eagle Bend in Lawrence. Courses in Burlington or Wichita. I don't go by myself often. I think golf is more fun when you have other people you play with. It's relaxing to be out on the course. You don't think about basketball. You think about playing golf.

That's kind of how I unwind. I'm not a partying kind of guy, so I didn't go out, although sometimes I would go out with the guys after a big win just to hang out. I wouldn't drink. I've watched a lot of movies. I've got my Hastings card. I'd go there and rent a bunch of movies and sometimes go to the movie theaters.

I don't mind doing things others might consider tedious.
I love seeing the finished product at the end.

As you can probably tell from my hobbies, I like things that take time. I enjoy the process, I enjoy the details and I love seeing a finished product. When I was in high school, I got into woodworking because we had a great teacher at Burlington named Doug Stewart. He's crazy talented. He carved a life-sized, 6'9" Larry Bird out of wood. He'll carve bears into tree trunks with a chain saw. He's amazing. I took his class as a sophomore and loved it. You'd start out making a clock or whatever everybody was making. But I took it as an independent study as a senior, meaning I had two-and-a-half hours per day to focus on woodworking projects.

I made a coffee table that is a replica of the Allen Fieldhouse court. It has all the lines on it, it has the Jayhawk, every little thing. I made it out of maple, so it would be an authentic basketball floor, then lacquered it so that it had the ever-important traction a basketball floor should have. For the legs, I cut a couple of rims in half and bolted them to the bottom, so that the half-circle of a rim swings out like a leg. I had all the coaches and players on the national championship team come to my room and sign it.

I also carved my sister a wooden Jayhawk. I just love seeing a finished product and I don't mind if it's tedious getting there. I guess it's like that saying, Rome wasn't built in a day.

I'm pretty content doing things like that. Probably to some people that sounds boring. They like to go out and party or whatever. I get that, and I don't have anything against it, necessarily. By that I mean I don't have anything against people who drink. I have no issue with it. It just isn't for me. As a Christian, it's a decision I've made in order to make sure I'm living for God. This isn't to say I haven't consumed alcohol. I have, and I can't stand the taste of it. I think beer tastes terrible. I'm not suggesting this is the main reason I don't drink, but the taste certainly did nothing to draw me to it.

—◆—

Tyrel's decision not to drink created an interesting dynamic for him and his friends and teammates, who observed that temperance is not necessarily an easy decision.

For one thing, since he wasn't a regular on the bar scene, whenever he did turn up, people noticed.

"Every once in a while he would come out and hang out with me and just stand around and have a pop," Welter said. "People wouldn't see him out very often, so when he was out, people loved to see him. They'd be taking pictures like crazy. There were a few times when maybe I was there for my birthday and he had come out to be a good friend. All the sudden, people would be buying him drinks like crazy. I don't know if they necessarily wanted to see him drunk. They probably did. He didn't even ask for them. They were just throwing them at him. He would give them to all of us, so it benefitted us. He would just say thank you and take a picture, but it wasn't his thing. It was crazy."

It also wasn't easy being the guy who abstained when others indulged.

"On weekends, he wouldn't be getting drunk, all those things," Lacie said. "He would be at home playing video games, drinking a Dr. Pepper. If you didn't know he was a basketball player, you would have never known he played sports.

"I think it was maybe hard at times. He wanted to be a good teammate, he wanted to fit in, he wanted to be friends with all of them. That's hard as an incoming freshman. A lot of times freshmen will do anything because they want to be like their teammates."

Aldrich sensed the same thing.

"He would go out with us once in a while, but he would never drink or do anything like that," Aldrich said. "He would always just hang out. We'd try to include him in conversations and all that. We didn't want to have him come out and sit in the corner. He's an outgoing guy. He knows a lot of people. I think it was hard, though, for him."

—◆—

It was never a struggle to not drink, but at the same time it's a very social activity. Like anybody else, I want to be part of what's going on. I want to be with my teammates or friends that may drink or go out. I want to be connected with them. It was tough sometimes knowing my friends or my teammates are out partying or whatever. But I didn't look at it as a bad thing. I'm not one to judge. I would say there is always a struggle in this world. You're always combating things you could do that are fun, or things you have done in the past. But you're doing this for your life and your relationship with Jesus. That was my whole mindset. That's what kept me on the path.

In college, everything is available to you. You're on your own. You can do whatever you want and no one will say anything against it. But that's just not the way I wanted to live. At first, my teammates probably didn't get that about me. But over time they realized I was a Christian and a party boy wasn't the way I wanted to be perceived. They were extremely accepting and encouraging.

A byproduct of it was that I felt like, by striving to live for the Lord, it kept me out of trouble. Not that I'm perfect. I have countless flaws and make a lot of mistakes in my life and will continue to do so. But having your focus on God instead of the things of this world will keep you from doing a lot of things that put you in the newspaper and get people saying bad things about you.

I don't want to say I'm proud of this because I know it's the life I'm supposed to lead and the one God has set forth for me. Regardless of how many temptations you're faced with, you always have the ability to go the opposite direction. I had failings in college and I did things I shouldn't have. But I always came back to Him. So I'm not proud of myself. I'm thankful to the Lord for his gift of forgiveness and for allowing me to live my life as a steward for Him.

I am reminded of one of my favorite Bible verses:

> *1 Corinthians 10:13. No temptation has seized you except what is common to man. And God is faithful; he will not let you be tempted beyond what you can bear. But when you are tempted, he will also provide a way out so you can stand up under it.*

I talked about these things with my teammates from time to time. Mostly about why I became a Christian. Most of them believe in the Lord, and I thought that was a really cool thing we had in common. If something was going on in their life, sometimes they would ask me to pray for them. I would lead us in prayer before every game. They all loved it, and I was honored to share the gospel with them.

I'd hate to sound preachy here. That's not my goal at all. And I don't want this to come off as though if you aren't living the same lifestyle I am, you aren't a Christian. You never know what's in a person's heart. That's truly the most important thing. They could live their life in a way you don't think is right, but they may have it in their heart they believe in the Lord and want to follow Him. Being a Christian isn't about what you do, it's about what's in your heart.

Most people who closely followed our team probably knew something about my faith, but one thing people probably would find unusual about me is that I don't watch that much sports on TV. I like watching basketball on TV. I don't like watching baseball on TV, although I do like going to games. I'm really not a big football fan. I'll watch people I know, like Darrell or Alonso, but not much beyond that. What I really love is soccer. I could watch it all day. It's such a team sport. I love it. I played until I was in sixth grade. I also love watching golf, just because those guys are so ridiculously good.

I am sure a lot of people are curious about just what it is like to be a Kansas basketball player on campus every day. I will do my best to explain it.

When you're walking around campus, people recognize you. I feel like I blend in at least a little bit, but if you're someone like Cole, who is 6'11", it's impossible to go unnoticed. You get some weird looks here and there, but most people just accept you as another student, which is great. I never had a student ask me for an autograph or anything during or after class.

Classmates will come up and congratulate you on a win the night before or whatever, and that's awesome. I've always thought it was really cool to be recognized and see how much students support Kansas athletics.

—◆—

Tyrel's pseudo-fame affected Welter's existence, too.

"We were at a concert in Kansas City, eating with his family," Welter said. *"A lot of people knew who he was and wanted to take pictures. All of a sudden they all wanted a picture with me. I think they thought I was on the team."*

Going places with Tyrel could be an issue, too.

"Sometimes it might take 20 minutes longer to get somewhere because people want autographs," Welter said. "I know he loves it. It's fun to watch."

Sometimes, the attention was astonishing.

"I saw a guy one time walk up and pretty much for 20 minutes tell him how much he loved him," Welter said. "He was at a barnstorming tour and a little kid started bawling in his arms. I think that put some perspective how much the game of basketball motivates people to want to be him. He's so modest, but honestly there's probably little kids now wanting to be Tyrel Reed. He shrugs that off."

—◆—

When you know people recognize you, it does affect your approach a little bit. I don't think I raised my hand one time in college. If called on, I would answer, but I never raised my hand. I was afraid people would be going, "That's a stupid question. What an idiot." There is a stigma with athletes in the classroom. I don't think college athletes are generally less intelligent than the rest of the student body, but some college athletes might not apply themselves in the classroom for various reasons.

With professors, you never really know what you're in for. Some of them are really cool with you being on the team and understanding you're going to be travelling and missing classes. They're fine with giving you an assignment ahead of time or understanding why you are going to miss class. Others, I think, are out to prove a point that you aren't entitled to anything because you're on the basketball team. They won't change things for you at all. You just deal with it.

My freshman year, I went to tutoring. Most players do that their whole time at KU, and it is a great way not only for the player to stay on top of things, but for the coaches to make sure they're on top of things. It can be a struggle. With a lot of guys, they make you come in for tutoring and you have to be there a certain amount of time, usually two hours per night. As you can imagine, this isn't much fun. The evenings are really the only time we have any free time and it kind of stinks when you have to attend tutoring. A lot of the disciplinary stuff you hear about that never gets explained has to do with tutoring and academic stuff. The school has to make sure we are all in good academic standing, because it can be penalized by the NCAA if we aren't.

—◆—

Because of directives from Self, players aren't supposed to talk to outsiders, even friends or relatives, about certain team issues.

Welter said co-workers and friends who knew he lived with Tyrel would often come to him looking for inside information. But he didn't have it.

"I wouldn't have much," he said. "He did what he needed to do. He followed that honor code as close as you could. I don't know if everybody followed it that closely, but he did a good job of it. Early on I might try to get something out of him. Once I realized I couldn't, I just let it be.

"He'd come home and you could tell when he was frustrated. He's about the most cheerful, upbeat guy in the world, but when he wanted to be by himself, I'd let him be. I knew something went down, but I didn't know what. Every once in a while I'd read the newspaper and see somebody got suspended or something. I knew he'd been running or something. I remember one time he had three practices in one day."

—◆—

Fortunately for me, I never had to deal with that. After my freshman year, my coaches trusted me that I was going to get my work

We have the best fans in the country, no doubt. I never got to do it, obviously, but I've sometimes thought about how fun it must be to be a KU student in the student section.

done. Never once did they ask me about school, which I'm sure was a good thing. I don't learn well through tutoring so it was nice when they said I could stop going. It goes better for me when I learn it in class or when I can take it home and figure it out myself. I spent a lot of time studying at the library, often after curfew. My coaches never questioned that was really what I was doing. If you can gain that trust, it makes things easier on you.

I was able to complete my degree in exercise science in three-and-a-half years, which some people seem to find surprising. The way it worked out was that I was able to get some college credit while I was still in high school, so I knocked out some of my general education classes before I got on campus. This meant that I got to start taking classes toward my major during my freshman year, and I took 17 or 18 hours per semester.

Incidentally, my freshman year was my most overwhelming year academically. This is because I took anatomy lab in the spring semester of that year. Normally I tried to take my more challenging classes in the fall semester, when we aren't travelling nearly as much. As you can imagine, lab courses are not really designed to be experienced from hotel rooms in places like Boulder, Colorado or San Antonio, Texas. You need to be there. You need to cut into the cadaver. You need to learn hands-on, step by step. And here I was, playing the longest basketball season possible, thinking, "Am I ever going to catch up?"

Fortunately, I had a great TA who was willing to let me come in on Saturdays and take quizzes or go through my lab work. It sucked going in on a Saturday, but at the same time, it was nice that somebody was willing to help you like that.

Scott "Scooter" Ward was also a huge part of it, not just for me, but for all of us. By title, he is our academic advisor, but he is so much more than that. Not only does he help us decide which classes to take and which major to choose, he works with teachers on our behalf, he tutors us sometimes, he's always there to help with a paper or help you get started with something. We have to take all our classes in the mornings so we can practice in the afternoons, too, and he's helpful in making that happen. He goes the extra mile.

Mario Little (right) and I took a photo with Scott "Scooter" Ward (with glasses), our academic and career counselor, at graduation. Scooter has a big job keeping us all in line academically, but goes beyond the call of duty.

Scooter has a great relationship with a lot of teachers on campus, so he sometimes will talk to them with us to figure things out. Most of the teachers are pretty good about working with us on account of our travel schedule. They'll let you turn in an assignment when you get back from a trip or over e-mail, although the best way to do it is to turn in your assignments before you leave. This is because there isn't a lot of free time on most of our road trips. We usually travel the day before the game, arrive, practice, eat, then crash. Next day is the game and we fly back right after it.

It's different during the Big 12 Tournament or the NCAA Tournament, when you're there for a few days. Scooter and a couple other academic support people will travel with us to make sure we keep on top of everything. It's a big job, making sure an entire basketball team stays eligible.

The other thing is that I learn better that way. I don't like to study, and I really didn't do as much studying as they tell you to do. I was just like anybody else. I never turned in work late or anything like that, but I would procrastinate sometimes. I probably studied three, four, maybe five hours per week, sometimes more. I learn best in the classroom. If I'm listening and writing it down, I tend to remember things better that way. I might have spent an hour per day just making sure I had everything done.

That changes some during finals week, and this is another time when being an athlete changes the way you prepare. If you're a regular student who doesn't work, you might be able to take an entire day and devote it to studying. I know a lot of people do it that way. You get started and you kind of get going and it works out. Well, we might be able to get started, but then we'll have to stop, go to practice, go lift weights and be away from it for four or five hours. I felt it was kind of hard to get started again after that. Even though we aren't playing games that week, we're still hitting it pretty hard with basketball.

But as you know by now, I'm not one to sit there for hours on end, either.

It was always a struggle for me to get started because I'd be doing 10 different things. Once I got started, it was just like anything else. Playing a video game, for example, I'll sit down and play it for an hour, then get bored and have to do something else. Studying was the same thing. I could sit down and be focused for a while, but then I'd have to get up and get something to eat or talk on the phone.

Generally speaking, I wouldn't say college was any more or less difficult than I expected it to be. When you're in high school you hear these horror stories about how much tougher it is, and it is tougher, but I felt like if you stayed on top of it, turned your stuff in and went to class, it was manageable, even if you are an athlete. It is a lot like the kids who have jobs in college. I always respected those kids who had to work and pay their own way. They have to work so hard and manage their time well. It's a lot like us. Being an athlete is our job.

It probably helped me that I knew what I wanted to study once I entered college. For most of high school I didn't know what I wanted to be, but then I hurt my ankle pretty badly my senior year. I had to go to a lot of physical therapy that season, and I realized I liked that. I liked helping people and seeing them get better. Plus, it played to my academic strengths. I've never been a big math guy. I mean, I can do math, but once you get past its practical usage, I don't like it much. My brain is wired for memorization, so that fit the sciences pretty well. In exercise science, it's a lot of memorization of body parts and things. That has always come to me fairly easily.

I have more KU gear than I know what to do with.
Also, note the fan: I've got to have some air moving when I sleep.

This isn't to say I didn't sometimes have to dive in pretty deep. If I had a big test or paper coming up, I would go to the library on campus. I found it easier to focus there than if I were at home. It helped, too, that I could meet some classmates there.

I don't really compare my academic career and my athletic career much. Both of them went well, but I don't think they're the same. I wouldn't say I was incredibly driven to succeed academically.

ACADEMIC ALL-AMERICANS

Bud Stallworth
Tom Kivisto
Cris Barnthouse
Ken Koenigs
Lynette Woodard
Darnell Valentine
David Magley
Angie Snider
Jacque Vaughn
Jerod Haase
Angie Halbleib
Ryan Robertson
Cole Aldrich
Tyrel Reed

I'm equally proud of the way my basketball and academic careers turned out. This honor sort of combines them.

Obviously, being the son of a couple of teachers, that was important in our household, but it wasn't something we talked a lot about.

I feel like, in general, whatever you're going to do, it says in the Bible, do everything as though you're not working for men, you're working for God. You may not want to do it but doing it for the Lord makes it that much easier. I wanted to do everything my best.

As it worked out, this sort of built up to my senior year, when I was named an Academic All-American. They send you a plaque for that and they put my name up on a hallway in the Fieldhouse the day after it was announced. That was really cool. The biggest honor, though, is that they put my name on a banner that hangs from the rafters in Allen Fieldhouse.

I definitely feel blessed I was given that opportunity to have my name up there and do well enough in school. It was awesome seeing Cole, who was my roommate the year before, become the Academic All-American of the Year and to follow him up. I wasn't quite as good as him, but that's OK with me. Coach Self was always very proud of me because it was academics and not just basketball. You can't put all your eggs in one basket.

One of the things I love about KU and Lawrence is how culturally diverse it is. I'm from a small town with probably a narrower worldview. In Lawrence, you get exposed to so many ideas. Even if they're things you disagree with, it's good to be confronted with those things. For example, in my philosophy class, everyone had their own beliefs. That was really interesting. That's one thing I look back on. I'm glad I came to a school like KU. You could go to other places where they're more set in their ways. KU is completely diverse.

My graduating class in Burlington was around 60 kids. You go to a class at KU where you have 1,000 kids in it at Budig Hall. I enjoyed that (even if I wasn't going to speak up in class).

One of the things that goes along with being noticed is being noticed by girls. Nobody doesn't like that. However, I consider myself fortunate that I had a girlfriend the whole time. I believe God put Jessica in my life to keep me on the right path. It was a good thing having her, because there are temptations every day. I'm human. I faced those things. But having Jessica to keep me grounded and knowing she was the one I wanted to be with made things that much easier.

—◆—

Tyrel is characteristically thrifty, though Welter said the one thing he will splurge on is Jessica.

"He wants to make her as happy as he can," Welter said. "He'll give in and spend a little bit more on her."

Otherwise, a certain cheapness and modesty defines Tyrel's expenditures. Even in Las Vegas, where Tyrel is a sneaky gambler.

"Instead of keeping your chips on the table, when he starts making money, you'll see him sliding those chips into his pocket," Welter said. "At the very end, I'd walk up to him and be like, 'How'd you do?' He'd say, 'Oh, I did OK.' Then you look down at his pocket and you see it's just bulging. You're like, 'You are such a liar.' He'd just smile and walk off. We call it rat-holing."

Anybody who knows him will also describe Tyrel as incredibly lucky.

"We'd take maybe $40 to the casino," Welter said. "It's pretty rare when he loses money at a casino. It's unreal. I'm not the only one who says that. His dad says the same thing. He's the luckiest kid I've ever seen. Last time we went, after the entire trip was all said and done, he ended up with his trip paid for. He did well."

Generally, Tyrel is described as being risk-averse. His wife says he drives "like a grandma," and he has never had a speeding ticket. But he will play a little blackjack, and he will take a car gleefully into the snow.

"He used to have a green Jetta," Welter said. "We'd go in big parking lots in the snow. He'd spin it around. That was one of the funniest things, taking that car out in the snow. It did really well, too, to get through some of those drifts we drove through on purpose. He kept it together. It was pretty funny. That was the one thing you'll see him do. I think he likes to drive through the snow. He sees it as a challenge."

—◆—

It wasn't always easy for Jessica. She had to be accepting of everything. I'm always taking pictures with other girls. Just fans, but still. It can be hard for a girlfriend to deal with that. She became very cool with it, very trusting.

I kept this pretty quiet, but I proposed to her in March. You could say I'm pretty young to be getting married, but it was a prayer thing. I prayed about that a lot. I felt God had placed her in my life. Two is better than one. I felt lucky to be with her. I enjoyed my times with her. It was never something that was forced or hard to do. Some people may think, "Well, you knew her in high school and started dating in college, so you never got to see anyone else or meet any other girls." I wouldn't say that. I still talk to other girls. I'm friends with other girls and know other girls. I felt like this was meant to be.

— ◆ —

Jessica, of course, accepted the proposal after a few years of being what you might call a Basketball Girlfriend, which is a little different from a regular girlfriend.

"I guess that's what you do after four years of dating," she said, joking. "My sister said it's because I'm a jersey-chaser. I think she's just jealous because she didn't get a basketball player. She got a golfer.

"He's a great guy. He's a great leader, spiritually, bringing out the best in people. He has the characteristic that ... not that he makes you a better person. I know that sounds super cheesy. But he really does bring out the best in you. He's extremely kind and thoughtful and very welcoming to people. When you're with him you're like, 'I can't be rude.' You feed off his characteristics."

Jessica was born and raised in Burlington. She first met Tyrel in junior high and was not attracted to him.

"One of my friends had a crush on him," she said. "I was like, 'Ew, he is weird. He has big ears. You are crazy.' He became friends with my cousin, who is a year older than me. I kind of got to know him. I was like, 'This kid's all right.' He's a good athlete and he seems OK. It was funny because I thought he was the weirdest kid. He was always super nice to me when he was hanging out with my cousin.

"He was a really goofy kid. He had a ton of energy. He was always doing weird things with his friends. You know how teenage boys are. He's got a goofy sense of humor."

While they were dating during college, Jessica had to deal with the reality that other girls were around, even if Tyrel wasn't interested in them.

"You trust him, but sometimes there are the girls out there you don't trust," she said. "There's one thing I find kind of annoying: We were at the grocery store the other day. There was this group of girls. You know how people try to pretend they're on their cell phone, but they're taking a picture of you? That kept happening. I wanted to be like, 'Just ask to take a picture. Don't be sneaky and creepy. It's really creeping me out.' That's one thing with girls. I really don't mind at all when they ask him to take pictures; I know he enjoys it and loves talking to fans.

"I knew he was faithful and I could trust him. It wasn't something I ever really worried about because of the guy he is. If he would have been a different way, I probably would have had a lot of issues with that. Sometimes they'll take a picture and I'll be like "That girl is totally hanging off of you. Not cool.' It's not something he can control."

—◆—

Being a basketball player at KU, people want to hang out with you; they want to see you, they watch you. It grants you access to a lifestyle you have to be careful with. Coach Self always says we live in a glass house. Whether you think they are or not, everyone is watching what you're doing. If you do something stupid, it's going to make the front page of the newspaper. If one of your friends does it, it's maybe a blurb on the fourth page that no one will ever read. You've got to be smart. Always stay on your guard a little bit.

Personally, I never felt like people wanted to test me but that was probably because I tried not to put myself in the kinds of situations where people try to test you. I'm sure there are people who are jealous of what some of those guys have. That's understandable. We receive a lot of things other people don't. We need to be thankful, but people might resent you for that.

People will come up to me at a restaurant and want to say hi, and I never felt annoyed by that. I loved it and encouraged it. I'm a normal kid and they want to talk to me, great. I thought that was cool. If you were Coach Manning, that might get old. I'm an unnoticeable guy. I look like everyone else. I like when fans come up to me and want to talk and tell stories or things they did at the national championship. That's one of the reasons it's fun to play. You hear how you may have brought joy to someone else's life.

You have to live on campus until your senior year. Whereas most kids go home for the summers, we have to stay in Lawrence to take summer classes and to work out. Most of us work camps, too. We basically get four weeks off per year, but only two of those are during the summer. For guys who live out of state, I think the school is allowed to pay for one trip home, usually over Christmas break. The rest of the time you're on your own.

Maybe this doesn't sound like much of an issue, and maybe it isn't, but we don't get paid and it's impossible for us to have jobs. I don't know what kind of job you could get that would allow you to maintain the kind of schedule we have to maintain. We get a stipend to cover living expenses, but otherwise our only income is from working basketball camps in the summer.

Those pay pretty well, but they have to pay you whatever the going rate is for an instructor at a camp. We're talking about maybe a couple thousand dollars if you work a lot of camps, which has to last you until the next summer. The best thing to do is save it. You could make more than that if you worked a ton of camps, but you also want to work on your game, too. The offseason is all about individual skills. If you need to work on your jumper or your ball handling or whatever, you spend the summer on that. It's also when you really get in the weight room and put on weight if you need to.

I always took the offseason as a break. You're able to work on the things you want to. Your weekends are usually off so you can go golf, hang out with friends, go to Kansas City. You can feel like a regular kid.

Teaching kids things like how to do layups is one of the only ways for a college basketball player to make extra money.

"For I know the plans I have for you," declares the LORD, "plans to prosper you and not to harm you, plans to give you hope and a future."

James 1:2

The Future

CHAPTER 9

People think I should be a coach, but at this point I just don't want to.

I'm not ruling that out, because I do love the game and I want to be around it. I'm just not sure I want the lifestyle a coach has to live. All the nights on the road recruiting, the countless hours at the facility. I don't know how all of our coaches do it. They truly love the game of basketball and are completely invested in their jobs. I want to see the world. I want to spend time with my family. I want to eat my wife's amazing cooking.

— ◆ —

Debbie Reed says she isn't sure Tyrel is well-suited to dealing with some of the personality issues coaches have to deal with.

"Tyrel really gets frustrated with teammates," she said. "He doesn't understand people not having that drive to go 100 percent all the time. That was probably his biggest frustration in college, was his teammates not practicing hard. He just never understood why anybody ever would do that. That's one reason he'll probably never coach basketball. Tyrel cannot handle people not giving 100 percent. Coaches have to put up with some of that, with personalities."

— ◆ —

I know I still want to play basketball. By the time this book comes out, I might have a team. I'm looking overseas and pretty much open to anything.

There is great basketball everywhere now. Everybody wants to play in some awesome country like Spain or Italy, but I'll go anywhere that's safe. I know my agent wouldn't let me go somewhere dangerous.

There's no telling how long I'll play. I could see playing for 10 years, but who knows? Maybe I'll get over there, hate it, and just hang 'em up. I've been accepted to KU Med. That acceptance is good for two years, so if I play longer than that I'll have to re-apply. I hope they take me back because I would like to eventually finish physical therapy school and someday open my own business. I'd like to work with athletes, if possible.

But my plans are really not plans. My plan is to go wherever and do whatever the Lord has in store for me. My wife and I are young with no plans to have kids anytime soon. This is the time in our lives we can do things like this. I'd love to see the world through basketball, but I'd also like to travel for fun, too. I don't even know where I want to be rooted. I love Lawrence, so I could see this area being kind of my home base, but who knows?

—◆—

There is a lot of newness in all this for Tyrel's family.

*"I'm excited we're getting to possibly explore a different place,"
Jessica said. "It's exciting we might be able to go to this new place and
not have any worries for a while. It's kind of scary not knowing our
future, but at the same time it's awesome letting it be in God's hands."*

*For Tyrel's parents, this means a new phase in life. For the last 20
years, their lives have revolved around sports. Workouts, practices,
games, events. Even most of their vacations somehow involved the kids
and their sports. But Lacie moved to San Diego in May and, after living
an hour and 10 minutes away for the last four years, Tyrel is shipping
off, too.*

"I always said I hate winter so bad," Debbie Reed said. "The only thing that's ever gotten me through winter is basketball. I hope my winter's not too long this year."

Stacy traveled to every game of his son's career, while Debbie missed just six. And they both did this while maintaining their teaching jobs. This sounds almost impossible, until Stacy deconstructs it.

"KU plays about 20 home games," he said. "So that's easy. Missouri is three hours. I can teach school, get there, turn around and drive back. Iowa State, Nebraska, Oklahoma State, and Oklahoma are the same way. The only games I ever had to take any time off were if they went somewhere like New York or L.A. or down to Texas. Then the tournament games were either in Oklahoma City or Kansas City. I drove a lot. I got home a lot of times very late at night."

When KU played at USC, Stacy flew to Los Angeles in the morning, watched the game, and flew back at night.

His travels were well-documented in the local media, but he felt bad Debbie didn't get as much credit for all her trips.

"It was 149 games of pure enjoyment for his dad and mom," Stacy said.

—◆—

Jessica is in the same boat I am with school. She majored in pre-occupational therapy, which is a little different than physical therapy. She deals more with helping people recover from strokes and things like that. We might end up going to medical school together. We both have three years of that ahead of us.

You get out of a small town and you start seeing the world, the people, the things. I want to see as much as I can. Cole said he thinks he can get me tickets to the Olympics next year. I'd like to go to a World Cup some day. Alonso Rojas's family is from Peru. He thought about going to the next World Cup and I told him to hit me up. If I'm not doing anything, I'd love to go.

I could see myself doing adventurous things. I don't want to be stupid. I'm not going to be doing Jackass stunts, but I could see running with the bulls in Spain or something. I love being active and feeling young.

I think I'd try foods. I'm OK with experimenting. Jessica is an amazing cook. Her brother was a chef and her whole family is full of amazing cooks. She'll talk your ear off about that. She wants to make me food every day. It makes her happy. I'll probably eat well the rest of my life.

—◆—

Jessica is of French and Irish heritage, but her family eats like Italians.

"My grandpa grew up in this poor Irish household on the East Coast," she said. "In his family, you had to work to eat meat. He grew up saying, 'I'm going to be a butcher when I grow up so my family has meat every night.' My family is all about the food."

She is almost embarrassed by it.

"My whole family – it's kind of sad – we live to eat," she said. "We live to cook, we live to eat. We have huge gatherings, but not to celebrate or anything. Mom was a stay-at-home mom. My brother went to culinary school. He's awesome. It's just a big part of our lives.

"It's one thing I'm passionate about and love. During finals, people might play video games or whatever to procrastinate. I might make a bunch of homemade cinnamon rolls so I don't have to do my work."

—◆—

We're definitely similar. I'd say she's more outgoing than I am. She's pretty athletic. She made it to state in track and triple jump. But she's more of a girly girl.

I think I'm going to remain competitive the rest of my life. I'm not planning on having kids any time soon, but whenever I do, I don't want them to feel forced to be an athlete or forced to play basketball. Whatever their talents are, I want to help them in that direction.

Jessica and I are both from Burlington, but we're more college sweethearts than high school sweethearts. When we were in junior high, she thought I was weird.

You can see we're both pretty happy in this photo. I know the Lord put Jessica in my life and I'm blessed to have her as my wife.

I won't be disappointed if they aren't basketball players. I want them to be good kids and have a heart for God. That's the main thing.

Probably at some point we'll have a 2008 team reunion. Maybe a 10-year thing. I haven't heard any talk about it yet, though. I still see a lot of those guys in the summers. They'll come back for Coach Self's camps, so those are good times to see everybody. I'm closer to some guys than others, obviously. Cole will be a friend forever. I'll stay in close contact with Conner, Chase, Brady, Mario Little, and Tyshawn. I still talk to the twins quite a bit.

Hopefully in a few years we'll all get together again. And hopefully by that point there will be some other kid who remembers hearing a specific song on his iPod on the way to play in the national championship game. A kid who worked his whole life to get to that point. A kid who got to stand on the stage and know what it feels like to win a national championship at the place he always dreamed of playing.

Somebody might even write a book about that.

"I will instruct you and teach you
in the way you should go;
I will counsel you
and watch over you"

Psalm 32:8

To Belgium (and beyond)

CHAPTER 10

I have seen my walls, and they are orange.

But as I write these words, I cannot describe myself as highly familiar with Verviers, Belgium, which is where I live now. Verviers is not a big city. There are 55,000 people here, eleven of whom are professional basketball players for a team called VOO Verviers-Pepinster.

I am one of those people.

About the name: VOO is a Belgian broadband company. The rest of it describes a location, sort of like Perry-Lecompton or Shawnee Mission.

As you might have imagined, the NBA lockout made this a difficult year for non-NBA players to find basketball work overseas. A lot of NBA guys took roster spots that otherwise might have gone to someone like me, so I feel blessed to have found a good team in a pleasant country. It was kind of a crazy summer for me because of all the uncertainty. When summer began, nobody knew exactly what was going to happen with the NBA, then the lockout started and that kind of changed everything. It created a big domino effect that took some time to sort itself out. I figured I would end up signing somewhere, but it probably took longer than it would have in most other years.

Jess and I were pretty much open to anything, so long as it was safe and the team and league were stable, and we feel like this worked out.

You probably know of some of my teammates. Mike Singletary, the big scorer from Texas Tech, is on my team. So are Devan Downey, a guard who scored a ton of points at South Carolina, and Jason Love, a big man from Xavier who was drafted by the Philadelphia 76ers. It's good basketball.

As I write this, we haven't played any games yet, although I am told the fans will pack our 3,000-seat arena for most games.

The quality of basketball over here is pretty good. We have some guys on my team who were really good college players in the U.S.

Basketball is pretty big here. I guess they bang on these drums and do all this crazy stuff, which is exciting. It's always more fun when people care. Certainly this is not like at KU, where everybody lives and breathes basketball, but I feel like I landed in a good spot.

For now, though, I can't tell you much about it. Basically, I signed my contract, packed up, flew to Belgium two days later and immediately launched into what amounts to another boot camp. I spend all day at the gym, go to bed, then start again in the morning. I can tell you I've had the waffles, which are awesome, and I've seen an awful lot of fountains.

I live right downtown in an apartment furnished by the team. They also provide us with a car, although I haven't gotten mine yet. My place is right next to one of my teammates, so I'll toss him a few bucks a month and leech his Internet connection. It isn't what you would describe as a luxurious lifestyle, but I have what I need.

The thing that stands out to me is just how old everything is. I guess it isn't something you think much about as an American, but the United States is extremely young compared to Europe. A lot of these buildings near me have been around for hundreds of years.

This certainly is a new experience for me, getting paid to play basketball. This is my job, now, which just feels different. I also, of course, am not Belgian, so there are some cultural adjustments to make. For example, very few people speak English here. You will run into some situations where people might be able to decipher enough words to figure out what you need, but having conversations with the locals isn't really on the table. They speak mostly French, which is actually a bit of a lucky break for me, because my wife, Jessica, studied French in high school. That has been helpful at places like the grocery store. It's nice that my coach, Aaron McCarthy, and a few of my teammates are American. The Belgians on my team speak some English too, so at least as far as basketball is concerned, we can all communicate with each other.

I don't know much about the history of Belgium, but I do know everything here seems really old, and there are tons of statues around town.

This is where I have spent most of my time.
It seats only about 3,000, but I'm told the fans will get after it.

I have spent so much time in the gym, that my acclimation to all of this has mostly happened on the basketball court. Jessica has been out and about a little more. She loves to cook, and she has had to adjust a little bit. It's a lot harder to cook over here because she can't read anything at the store. Portions are smaller here, too, and things are more expensive. You have to save money and be as smart with it as you can and still get what you need.

I still kind of feel like a tourist. We went to a nearby McDonald's recently, and I had to just point at the menu to communicate what I wanted.

I recently went to the downtown area, where there are a lot of stores and little shops. Just walked streets a few times after practices. It's all very pretty, and very green. It rains a lot here. It rains for like 30 minutes really hard and then the skies will clear up. It won't be blue skies but it won't be raining, either. I'm not used to it raining all the time and being gloomy, so that's an adjustment, too.

As far as my role on the team, I don't know much yet. We have a scrimmage coming up, so I suppose I'll learn some more about it at that point, but I really am just living day by day. I have a schedule and I follow the schedule, go home to my wife, then follow my schedule again.

I can't tell for sure how "famous" the basketball players are in this town. I think the people who care about basketball know who my teammates and I are, but people on the street wouldn't know me from anybody else. I look like any other white European guy.

We may wear uniforms with sponsor logos on them over here, and I might not speak the local language, but at a certain point, basketball is just basketball.

If I'm walking around with my teammates in our practice gear, people figure it out, especially if Jason is around. People tend to notice a 6-10 guy.

I am starting to feel like I live here a little bit. I say bon jour and I say merci, and I go to the gym.

AFTERWORD
By Tully Corcoran

Maybe you can say Dean Smith was a small-town Kansas kid who did well at KU. He was kind of from Emporia and kind of from Topeka, but in either case was from somewhere significantly bigger than Burlington.

Adolph Rupp was from Halstead, which is about Burlington's size. He played at KU in 1922 and 1923. Arthur Lonborg, of Horton, was an All-American the same year World War I ended. Otto Schnellbacher was from Sublette. His run came in the late 1940s.

The point is, if you're looking for a modern (read: living) representative of small-town Kansas basketball at the state's biggest basketball power, you're looking for Tyrel Reed.

Because of Kansas' vast expanse of red barns and basketball heritage at its flagship institution, a lot of people think Kansas is like Indiana (or at least the cinematic version of it), churning out reams of farm-boy basketball players who set good screens, part their hair on the side, stick the open jumper, and turn into the local-boy-done-good at the big school on the hill.

But that just isn't it. My first hometown is Hutchinson, which is roughly 15 times the size of Burlington, and to my knowledge, has not produced a college basketball player of any real significance in my lifetime. My second hometown, Burrton, is less than half the size of Burlington and, to my knowledge, has not produced a person taller than 5'11" in my lifetime.

The point is, this doesn't happen. Tyrel Reed doesn't just happen. If the process of doing this book with him has shown me one thing, that is it.

I write about athletes for a living. High school, college, and professional athletes. I have always assumed I had a pretty good idea what it took. The best athletes are genetically blessed and psychologically driven. Mark Mangino, the former Kansas football coach, once was asked what made him so focused on the present moment, why he never looked ahead to dream or looked back to relish.

"Character flaw," he said.

There is something to that. The best athletes and the best coaches are the best because they care the most. Because they celebrate less and work more. Because knocking down one goal just clears the path for the next one. Sometimes being successful means being irrational.

These are things we know, things I could have described on an intellectual level. But talking to Tyrel and his family brought my understanding of this to a new level. There are a lot of good little ballplayers in Kansas. Curt Welter, another small-town kid (Hill City) who lived with Tyrel their senior year in college, was one of those guys.

"I was pretty good for our area," he said. "Just seeing the difference between me and him, it takes a lot to play at the University of Kansas."

Maybe you think you were a pretty good player. Maybe you think you could hold your own in a Big 12 game. Maybe you think if all you had to do was find an open spot and knock down the three, you could make it. Well, let me ask you this: When you're all alone in an empty gym, and you shoot 100 threes, how many do you make? Because Tyrel Reed makes 80 of them. On the run. All the time. You think you're athletic? Tyrel Reed can jump over your moderately sized late-model sedan.

Certainly, there is a lot of good fortune in this. The son of average-sized parents grew to 6'3". The leaping ability was always there. The competitiveness grew inside him.

But that would not have been enough. As you've seen from reading this book, this is a kid who devoted his life to being a good basketball player. He could make 25 consecutive free throws in fourth grade. Every morning for six years in junior high and high school he got up at 6 a.m. to work on his game and for three years of that drove 70 minutes each way to work on his body after school. Who as a scared freshman in high school went to Lawrence to play pickup games with the Jayhawks.

There was good fortune involved, but it was no accident he became the player he did.

I am sure reading these words will make him uncomfortable. You know from reading this book he doesn't like to talk about how good he is or the virtues he possesses or what remarkable things he has done. In all honesty, as a beat writer who covered him for four years, I found his humility to be both admirable and frustrating. When the kid from Kansas buries the dagger at Missouri, you're hoping for something a little more bombastic than that he was open and his teammates found him.

"My favorite Tyrel memory comes from a game his sophomore year at Nebraska," said Brady McCollough, who covers Kansas for *The Kansas City Star.* "Kansas was losing by two late, and Tyrel nailed back-to-back threes to give KU a four-point lead, and it was clear that Tyrel had mouthed off to Nebraska's Cookie Miller. As a beat writer on deadline, this was, like, awesome. It was his first year as a contributor, so we didn't quite know him that well yet, and we were hopeful that he would give us some insight or a good nugget. Turned out, Tyrel said he didn't know what he said to Cookie, and the quote I used from him was 'Just in the heat of battle.' Looking back, the moment was classic Tyrel. He rarely delivered great insight publicly, but you could learn everything you needed to know about him by watching him in moments like that."

That's him. Tyrel doesn't seem to consider himself remarkable, even though so many around him do. This has a lot to do with his father, Stacy, who always reminded him he didn't need to tell anybody what he had done. But Stacy in more recent years has tried to help his son develop a new perspective.

"I pushed him to understand that you're one of the first kids ever to represent small-town Kansas," he said. "He doesn't look at it like that. Being a coach for as long as I was a coach and being around it as long as I've been around sports, with my dad being a coach and being around sports for 35 years, I understood what small-town Kansas was all about. … He doesn't look at it like that."

Because he was an Academic All-American as a senior, his name now hangs from the rafters at Allen Fieldhouse. One of the last times we talked for this book, I asked him what he thought it would be like to one day take his kid there, point up at the rafters and say, "There's your daddy's name."

"Hopefully they don't erase it," he said.

APPENDIX

Quick Shots with Tyrel

- Favorite vacation spot ... Aruba
- Favorite breakfast spot in Lawrence ... Teller's
- Favorite lunch spot in Lawrence ... Pizza Shuttle
- Favorite dinner spot in Lawrence ... Paisano's
- The one dish in Lawrence you will miss most ... Pizza Shuttle. $4.75 walk-in special. Best deal in town.
- Favorite restaurant in Burlington ... My House (haha)
- Favorite genre of music ... Christian
- Least favorite genre of music ... Punk Rock
- Favorite movie genre ... Comedy
- Favorite TV show ... Seinfeld
- Favorite actor ... Adam Sandler
- Celebrity crush ... Cameron Diaz
- Most recent book you read ... Coach Wooden: One on One
- Sporting event you'd most like to attend ... FIFA World Cup
- What was your best performance at KU? My best all-around game would probably be the Cal game. Statistically speaking, that's it.
- Who was your funniest teammate? Mario Little.
- Best dunk by a teammate? Marcus' over the Pitt State guy. I felt bad for that guy.

- Biggest shot you made in your career ... The one against Cornell. We couldn't get over the hump that game, and that would have been a bad loss to have at home.
- Beach or mountains ... Mountains
- Big city loft or spacious suburban home ... Spacious suburban home
- Coffee or Red Bull ... Neither
- Biggie or Tupac ... Tupac
- Leno or Letterman ... Leno
- Conan or Kimmell ... Conan
- SUV, sports car or convertible ... Whichever gets best gas mileage
- Barbecue is best with beef or pork ... pork
- Do you believe in ghosts? No
- Aliens? No
- The Loch Ness Monster? Yes
- Favorite class ... Anatomy
- Favorite burger ... Buddy's Bar and Grill right outside of Burlington
- Favorite sandwich ... Quizno's

Tyrel Reed honors and accomplishments

- Career record of 132-17 makes him the winningest player in Kansas basketball history.
- First-team Academic All-American (2011)
- Three-time first-team Academic All-Big 12
- No. 9 on KU's all-time three-point makes list (176)
- All-Big 12 honorable mention (2011)
- Danny Manning "Mr. Jayhawk" Award (2011)
- Lowe's Senior CLASS first-team All-American (2011)
- Co-SIDA Academic All-District 7 (2011)
- Athletic Director's and Big 12 Commissioner's Honor Rolls (seven times)
- Mr. Kansas Basketball and Kansas Gatorade Player of the year (2007)

Career statistics

	Min	Pts.	Reb.	Ast.	To.	Stl.	Blk.	FG	3PT.	FT
2007-08	6.3	2.0	0.4	0.9	0.2	0.3	0.0	.514	.458	.000
2008-09	20.7	6.5	1.9	1.1	1.0	0.7	0.0	.407	.389	.825
2009-10	15.6	5.1	1.4	1.1	0.4	0.8	0.1	.496	.473	.833
20010-11	28.7	9.7	3.1	1.7	0.9	1.5	0.2	.408	.379	.798

There are a lot of reasons to come to Kansas, but none bigger than this. You're going to win championships. We had an awesome run in my four years there, and as I've said so many times, it was an amazing blessing to be a part of it.

ABOUT THE AUTHORS

Tyrel Reed

Tyrel won more games in a Kansas uniform than anybody in history. Between the regular season and conference tournament, he competed for eight Big 12 championships in his career, and won seven of them, finishing with a career record of 132-17.

On a team that went 35-3 in 2010-11, Tyrel was the only player to start all 38 games, averaging 9.7 points and 3.1 rebounds per game as a senior. His name now hangs on a banner in the rafters at Allen Fieldhouse, as he was named an Academic All-American as a senior. After graduating in three-and-a-half years with a degree in exercise science, he was accepted to the University of Kansas School of Medicine.

Tyrel grew up the younger of two kids in Burlington, Kansas, where he was named Mr. Kansas Basketball as a senior.

Tully Corcoran

Tully spent eight years at *The Topeka Capital-Journal,* the last four of which he spent as the newspaper's KU beat writer. His work has been honored many times by the Kansas Press Association.

He and his wife, Abby, live in Houston, Texas, where he works for Fox Sports Houston. This is his first book.